TEST PREP READING BOOK FOR CASAS READING STEPS LEVEL A—FORMS 621R AND 622R

Turning Learners into Proficient Readers while Preparing them for CASAS Reading STEPS Level A—Forms 621R & 622R

By

COACHING FOR BETTER LEARNING

TABLE OF CONTENTS

PREFACE

Dear Instructors,

Get ready to transform your ESL classroom with our *Test Prep Reading Book for CASAS Reading STEPS Level A,* specifically designed for the Form 621R and 622R reading comprehension tests. This essential tool aligns with the English Language Proficiency Standards (ELPS) for Adult Education. It satisfies the National Reporting System (NRS) and Workforce Innovation and Opportunity Act (WIOA) expectations, ensuring your ESL students are on the path to success.

This reading textbook is more than just a teaching aid; it is a comprehensive program tailored to bolster reading comprehension among ESL learners. With a structured layout of six units, 16 learner-centered reading lessons, and one practice test, your students will navigate essential topics like basic communication, consumer economics, community resources, health, employment, government, and law.

Leverage Bloom's Taxonomy's six levels of objectives and competencies (remembering, understanding, applying, analyzing, evaluating, and creating) to enhance your teaching methods. Each lesson in the book is a stepping stone that equips you with the strategies to teach reading effectively, focusing on important skills such as identifying main ideas, uncovering details, making inferences, summarizing content, applying knowledge, understanding the author's perspective, and contextual vocabulary. The clarity and depth of the lessons will enable you to deliver content that resonates with your students and solidifies their understanding.

Finally, this textbook isn't just about reading—it's about providing your students with the academic and life skills they need to thrive. As they progress through the book, they'll gain valuable insights and abilities to navigate the complexities of community life, family responsibilities, and the workplace. By using this book, you'll be equipping your students for standardized testing and real-world challenges.

INTRODUCTION

Dear Students,

This book will help you get ready for the CASAS Reading STEPS level A test. It's filled with lessons to help you read better.

The book has six units and one practice test. Each unit has two to three lessons, with 16 lessons in total. The lessons teach important skills like basic communication, understanding money, finding community help, staying healthy, finding a job, and learning about government and laws. These skills will help you in many parts of your life.

When you read this book, you will read different kinds of texts. They will have information about reading and real-world activities. After you read each text, you will answer questions. These questions make sure you understand the main points, details, the writer's thoughts, and the words they use.

Remember, reading gets better the more you do it. This book will help you in school, in your community, with your family and at work.

Good luck! Every lesson you finish will take you closer to your goals.

Reading Strategies:

Here are ten ways you can improve your reading comprehension skills:

1. Look at titles and subtitles to get an idea of what you will read.

2. Think about why you are reading. Is it to answer a question or learn something new?

3. Read out loud every day. The more you read, the better you will get.

4. Use pictures to help you understand the text.

5. Read again if you don't understand something.

6. Summarize. After reading, tell yourself what the text was about.

7. Ask questions. While reading, ask, "Who, what, where, when, why, and how?"

8. Connect the text to your own life or things you know.

9. Guess what the author means from clues in the text.

10. If you don't know a word, look it up in the dictionary.

Vocabulary Building:

Here are seven ways to learn more words:

How to Learn	What to Do
Find synonyms.	Look for words that mean the same as new words.
Use the words.	Try to use new words in your own sentences.
Make flashcards.	Write new words and their meanings on cards.
Create a vocabulary journal.	Keep a notebook with new words and their meanings.
Read regularly.	The more you read, the more words you will learn.
Learn word parts.	Study word beginnings (prefixes), endings (suffixes), and roots to understand more words.
Play word games.	Games like crosswords can help you learn new words.

Keep going! You can do it!

Lesson 1: Interactions with People

Objectives:

1. Students will read short texts and answer questions about interpersonal interactions.
2. Students will use new words to complete sentences about interacting with others.

Exercise 1- What do you see in the picture?

Exercise 2- Draw a line connecting each word to its meaning.

Word	Meaning
Greet	To come into the presence of someone
Introduce	To hold someone's hand and move it up and down
Discuss	To make someone known to others
Shake hands	To say hello or welcome someone
Meet	To talk about a topic

Exercise 3- Read the sentences below before answering the questions.

Anna and Luis

1. Anna and Luis are at a meeting.
2. They smile and shake hands.
3. Anna talks to Luis about their project.
4. They are working together.

Comprehension Questions:

1. Where are Anna and Luis?

2. What does Anna talk about?

3. How do they greet each other?

4. Are they happy to work together?

John and Emily

1. John and Emily are in a classroom.
2. John introduces himself to Emily.
3. They sit down and share ideas.
4. They are classmates.

Comprehension Questions:

1. Who are in the classroom?

2. What does John do first?

3. What do they do together?

4. What is their relationship?

Exercise 5- Read the dialogue below before answering the questions.

Sarah and Carlos

Sarah: Hi, my name is Sarah. What is your name?
Carlos: Hello, I am Carlos. Nice to meet you.
Sarah: Nice to meet you too, Carlos. Where do you work?
Carlos: I work at a restaurant in the city.

Comprehension Questions:

1. Who does Sarah meet?

____

2. What does Sarah ask Carlos?

____

3. Where does Carlos work?

____

4. What is in the city?

____

Exercise 6- Read the dialogue below before answering the questions.

Mike and Emily

Mike: Hello, my name is Mike.
Emily: Hi Mike, I am Emily.
Mike: Do you work here, Emily?
Emily: Yes, I am a teacher.

Comprehension Questions:

1. What is the man's name?

____

2. Who is the woman?

____

3. What question does Mike ask Emily?

____

4. What is Emily's job?

____

Exercise 7- Fill in the blanks with the correct words (*introduce, discuss, shake, greets, meet*).

1. Anna and Luis _______ hands when they meet.

2. Emily wants to _______ herself to the new group.

3. Mike likes to _______ ideas with his friends.

4. They _______ for the first time at the office.

5. Sarah _______ everyone at the event.

Exercise 8- Complete the sentences with your personal information.

1. My name is _______________.

2. I am from _______________.

3. I work as a _______________.

4. I like to _______________.

5. My favorite place is _______________.

Exercise 9- Dictation

Your teacher will read some of the new words from Exercise 2. Write down what you hear.

____

____

ANSWER KEYS

Exercise 2- Vocabulary Matching:
1. Greet - To say hello or welcome someone
2. Introduce - To make someone known to others
3. Discuss - To talk about a topic
4. Shake hands - To hold someone's hand and move it up and down
5. Meet - To come into the presence of someone

Exercise 3- Text 1:
1. They are at a meeting.
2. She talks about their project.
3. They shake hands.
4. Yes, they are happy.

Exercise 4- Text 2:
1. John and Emily are in the classroom.
2. John introduces himself.
3. They share ideas.
4. They are classmates.

Exercise 5- Dialogue 1:
1. Sarah meets Carlos.
2. She asks Carlos what he does.
3. Carlos works at a restaurant.
4. The restaurant is in the city.

Exercise 6- Dialogue 2:
1. The man's name is Mike.
2. Her name is Emily.
3. Mike asks Emily if she works there.
4. She is a teacher.

Exercise 7- Fill-in-the-Blanks:
1. shake
2. introduce
3. discuss
4. meet
5. greets

Lesson 2: Personal Information

Objectives:

1. Students will read short texts and answer questions about basic personal information.
2. Students will use new words to complete sentences about personal information and documents.

Exercise 1- What do you see in the picture?

Exercise 2- Draw a line connecting each word to its meaning.

Word	Meaning
Passport	The information that tells where you live
ID Card	A book used to travel to different countries
Address	A card that shows you are a student at a school
License	A card that shows who you are
Student ID	A card that shows you can drive a vehicle

Exercise 3- Read the text below before answering the questions.

A United States Passport

This is a passport. A man is holding the passport. The passport is from the United States. It helps him travel to different countries.

Comprehension Questions:

1. What is the man holding?

____

2. Which country is the passport from?

____

3. What does a passport help you do?

____

4. What is the author talking about?

____

Exercise 4- Read the text below before answering the questions.

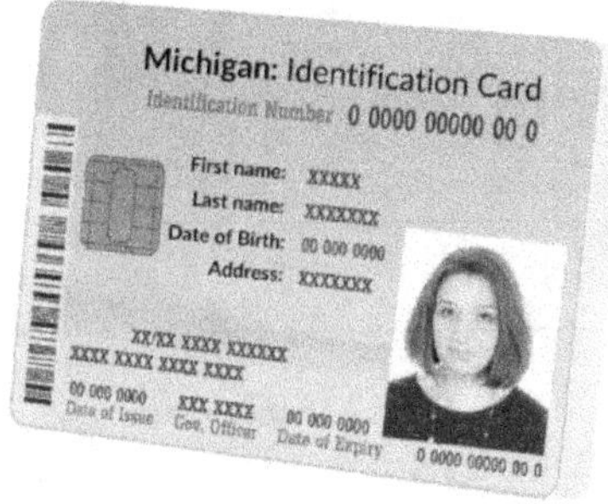

A State ID Card

This is a state ID card. It has a person's name, photo, date of birth and address. A state ID helps people know who you are. Many adults have a state ID.

Comprehension Questions:

1. What kind of card is this?

____

2. What information is on the card?

____

3. What is the purpose of a state ID?

____

4. Who might have a state ID?

____

Exercise 5- Fill in the blanks with the correct words (ID card, passport, address, license, student ID)

1. My name is on my ____________.

2. I need my ____________ to drive a car.

3. I can travel to Mexico with my ____________.

4. The ____________ shows I study at a school.

5. My ____________ tells people where I live.

Exercise 6- Complete the sentences with your personal information.

1. My name is ____________.

2. I live at ____________.

3. My ID number is ____________.

4. I have a ____________ card.

5. My student ID number is ____________.

Exercise 7- Dictation

Your teacher will read some of the new words from Exercise 2. Write down what you hear.

____

____

ANSWER KEYS

Exercise 2- Vocabulary Matching:

1. Passport - A book used to travel to different countries
2. ID Card - A card that shows who you are
3. Address - The information that tells where you live
4. License - A card that shows you can drive a vehicle
5. Student ID - A card that shows you are a student at a school

Exercise 3- Text 1:

1. The man is holding a passport.
2. The passport is from the United States.
3. It helps you travel to different countries.
4. The author is talking about a man with a passport.

Exercise 4- Text 2:

1. It is a state ID card.
2. A person's name, photo, date of birth and address are on the card.
3. It shows who a person is.
4. Many adults have state IDs.

Exercise 5- Fill-in-the-Blanks:

1. ID card
2. license
3. passport
4. student ID
5. address

REFLECTION ON LEARNING

Answer the following questions and discuss your responses with your teacher or classmates.

1. What reading strategies did you learn or practice in this unit?

2. What new words did you learn?

3. What reading challenges did you face?

4. What reading strategies do you need to improve?

5. What do you want your teacher to know?

Lesson 1: Using Money

Objectives:

1. Students will read short texts and answer questions on consumer economics and money.
2. Students will use new words to complete sentences about consumer economics and money.

Exercise 1- What do you see in the pictures?

Exercise 2- Draw a line connecting each word to its meaning.

Word	Meaning
Coin	To get something by paying money for it
Dollar	The amount of money something costs
Buy	A round piece of metal used to pay for things
Price	A paper showing what was bought and how much was paid
Receipt	Paper money used in the United States

Exercise 3- Read the text below before answering the questions.

Using Coins

This is a coin. It is small and round. People use coins to buy small things. Maria has a coin.

Comprehension Questions:

1. What is in the picture?

2. Is the coin big or small?

____

3. What can you do with a coin?

____

4. Who has a coin?

____

Exercise 4- Read the text below before answering the questions.

Dollar Bills

These are dollar bills. They are paper money. People use dollar bills to buy things. David has many dollar bills.

Comprehension Questions:

1. What is in the picture?

____

2. What kind of money is it?

____

3. What do people do with dollar bills?

____

4. Who has many dollar bills?

____

Exercise 5- Read the Receipt from BTEX Store before answering the questions.

BTEX Store Sale Receipt	
Item	**Price**
Bread	$2.00
Milk	$1.50
Apples (3)	$3.00
Total	$6.50

Comprehension Questions:

1. How much was the bread?

____

2. How many apples were bought?

____

3. What was the total price?

____

4. What was the most expensive item?

____

Exercise 6- Read the coupon from Foodlink Grocery Store before answering the questions.

Item	Discount
Any Fruit	10% off
Bread	Buy 1 Get 1 Free

Comprehension Questions:

1. What is the discount on fruit?

____

2. What is the special deal for bread?

____

3. Where is the coupon from?

____

4. Can you buy vegetables with this coupon?

____

Exercise 7- Fill in the blanks with the correct words (coin, price, buy, receipt, dollar).

1. A _______ is used to pay for small things.

2. You need a _______ to see how much you paid.

3. I want to _______ a book at the store.

4. A _______ is paper money in the US.

5. The _______ of the apple is $1.

Exercise 8- Complete the sentences with the appropriate words.

1. I have _______ coins in my pocket.

2. My favorite thing to buy is a _______.

3. The _______ of a bus ticket is $2.

4. At the store, I pay with a _______.

5. After shopping, I get a ____.

Exercise 9- Dictation

Your teacher will read some of the new words from Exercise 2. Write down what you hear.

____

____

ANSWER KEYS

Exercise 2- Vocabulary Matching:

1. Coin - A round piece of metal used to pay for things
2. Dollar - Paper money used in the United States
3. Buy - To get something by paying money for it
4. Price - The amount of money something costs
5. Receipt - A paper showing what was bought and how much was paid

Exercise 3- Text 1:

1. A coin is in the picture.
2. The coin is small.
3. You can buy small things.
4. Maria has a coin.

Exercise 4- Text 2:

1. Dollar bills are in the picture.
2. They are paper money.
3. They buy things.
4. David has many dollar bills.

Exercise 5- Receipt:

1. The bread is $2.00.
2. Three apples were bought.
3. The total was $6.50.
4. Apples were the most expensive item.

Exercise 6- Coupon:

1. 10% is the discount.
2. Buy 1 Get 1 Free.
3. The coupon is from Foodlink Grocery Store.
4. No, it is for fruit and bread.

Exercise 7- Fill-in-the-Blanks:

1. Coin
2. Receipt
3. Buy
4. Dollar
5. Price

Lesson 2: Buying Goods and Services

Objectives:

1. Students will read short texts and answer questions about purchasing goods and services.
2. Students will use new words to complete sentences about goods and services.

Exercise 1- What do you see in the pictures?

Exercise 2- Draw a line connecting each word to its meaning.

Words	Meaning
Goods	The amount of money you must pay
Bill	Things you buy, like food and clothes
Purchase	A place where you pay for goods
Service	Work or help you pay for
Register	To buy something

Exercise 3- Read the sentences below before answering the questions.

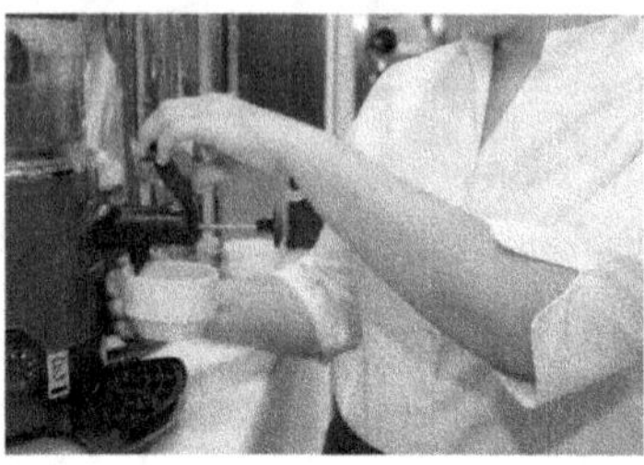

At a Café

1. Joe goes to a café.
2. He orders a coffee.
3. The waiter gives him a receipt.
4. The receipt shows the cost of the coffee.

Comprehension Questions:

1. Where does Joe go?

   a) Home
   b) At a café
   c) At the store

2. What does Joe order?

   a) Tea
   b) Water
   c) Coffee

3. Who gives Joe the receipt?

    a) Waiter
    b) Chef
    c) Cashier

4. What is on the receipt?

    a) Joe's name
    b) The cost of the coffee
    c) Joe's address

Exercise 4- Read the sentences below before answering the questions.

Buying Groceries

1. Anna buys groceries from a store.
2. She keeps the receipts to check later.
3. The receipts are for fruits and bread.
4. She keeps them in her wallet.

Comprehension Questions:

1. What does Anna buy?

    a) Clothes
    b) Groceries
    c) Furniture

3. What items are on the receipts?

    a) Fruits and bread
    b) Shoes and socks
    c) Books and pens

2. Why does Anna keep the receipts?

    a) To throw away
    b) To check later
    c) To give to a friend

4. Where does Anna keep the receipts?

    a) Bag
    b) Pocket
    c) Wallet

Exercise 5- Read the Electric and Gas Bill before answering the questions.

BTEL Energy Company Bill
Account Name: John Smith
Electricity Cost: $45
Gas Cost: $30
Due Date: 25th of the month

Comprehension Questions:

1. What is the name on the bill?

    a) Anna Lee
    b) John Smith
    c) Maria Scott

2. How much does the electricity cost?

    a) $20
    b) $30
    c) $45

3. How much does the gas cost?

    a) $25
    b) $30
    c) $35

4. What is the due date?

    a) 20th of the month
    b) 25th of the month
    c) 30th of the month

Exercise 6- Read the TowerApt Announcement before answering the questions.

TowerApt Apartment Available
Location: 123 Main St., Apt. 2
Rent Cost: $700 per month
Utilities Included: Water, Gas
Contact: 555-1234

Comprehension Questions:

1. Where is the apartment located?

    a) 456 Elm St.
    b) 789 Oak St.
    c) 123 Main St.

3. What utilities are included?

    a) Internet
    b) Water, Gas
    c) Electricity

2. How much is the rent?

    a) $500
    b) $700
    c) $900

4. What is the contact number?

    a) 555-4321
    b) 555-6789
    c) 555-1234

Exercise 7- Read the Cable and Internet Bill before answering the questions.

TVTex Corp Cable & Internet Bill
Account Name: Lucy Brown
Cable Cost: $50
Internet Cost: $35
Total Due: $85

Comprehension Questions:

1. Who is the bill for?

   a) Lucy Brown
   b) John Miller
   c) Anna Green

2. How much does the cable cost?

   a) $40
   b) $50
   c) $60

3. What is the cost of the internet?

   a) $25
   b) $35
   c) $45

4. What is the total amount due?

   a) $75
   b) $85
   c) $95

Exercise 8- Read the Receipt from BuilderShop Hardware Store.

Item	Quantity	Price per Item	Total Price
Hammer	1	$10	$10
Nails	1 box	$5	$5
Paint	2 cans	$8	$16
Total			$31

Comprehension Questions:

1. What is the total cost?

   a) $20
   b) $25
   c) $31

2. What is the cost of the nails?

   a) $5
   b) $10
   c) $15

3. Which item costs $8 each?

   a) Nails
   b) Hammer
   c) Paint

4. Where is the purchase from?

   a) A grocery store
   b) A hardware store
   c) A bookstore

Exercise 9- Fill in the blanks with the correct words (bill, purchase, service, items, cost).

1. You pay for a _______ when someone fixes your car.

2. The _______ is due at the end of the month.

3. I will _______ a new book today.

4. The _______ of the pen is $2.

5. The register has all the _______ listed.

ANSWER KEYS

Exercise 2- Vocabulary Matching:

1. Goods – Things you buy, like food and clothes
2. Bill – The amount of money you must pay
3. Purchase – To buy something
4. Service – Work or help you pay for
5. Register – A place where you pay for goods.

Exercise 3- Text 1:

1. b) Café
2. c) Coffee
3. a) Waiter
4. b) The cost of the coffee

Exercise 4- Text 2:

1. b) Groceries
2. b) To check later
3. a) Fruits and bread
4. c) Wallet

Exercise 5- BTEL Energy Company Bill

1. b) John Smith
2. c) $45
3. b) $30
4. b) 25th of the month

Exercise 6- TowerApt Announcement

1. c) 123 Main St.
2. b) $700
3. b) Water, Gas
4. c) 555-1234

Exercise 7- Cable and Internet Bill

1. a) Lucy Brown
2. b) $50
3. b) $35
4. b) $85

Exercise 8- BuilderShop Hardware Store Receipt

1. c) $31
2. a) $5
3. c) Paint
4. b) Hardware store

Exercise 9- Fill-in-the-Blanks:

1. service
2. bill
3. purchase
4. cost
5. items

Lesson 3: Household Finances and Budgeting

Objectives:

1. Students will read short texts and answer questions about managing household finances and budgeting.
2. Students will use new words to complete sentences about household finances and budgeting.

Exercise 1- What do you see in the picture?

Exercise 2- Draw a line connecting each word to its meaning.

Word	Meaning
Budget	Money set aside for future use
Rent	Money spent on things or bills
Savings	Money earned from work or a business
Expenses	A record of income and expenses
Income	Money paid regularly to live in a house or apartment

Exercise 3- Read the sentences below before answering the questions.

Paying Taxes

1. John looks at his tax papers.
2. He calculates his income for the year.
3. He writes down his expenses.
4. He plans to save money this year.

Comprehension Questions:

1. What is John looking at?

2. What does he calculate?

____

3. What does he write down?

____

4. What is his plan?

____

Exercise 4- Read the sentences below before answering the questions.

Bank Cards

1. Maria has a wallet with cards.
2. She carries her debit and credit cards.
3. She pays her rent using a card.
4. She saves some money each month.

Comprehension Questions:

1. What does Maria have?

____

2. What types of cards does she carry?

____

3. What does she pay with her card?

____

4. What does she do each month?

____

Exercise 5- Read the Rent Bill before answering the questions.

Rent Bill: ApartmentEx Company

Description	Amount
Rent	$1,200
Due Date	1st of every month
Late Fee	$50 if paid late

Comprehension Questions:

1. What is the amount of rent?

____

2. When is the rent due?

____

3. Is there a fee for late payment?

____

4. What company sends the bill?

____

Exercise 6- Read the household budget before answering the questions.

Household Budget Table

Category	Amount
Income	$2,500
Rent	$1,000
Food	$400
Utilities	$200
Savings	$300

Comprehension Questions:

1. What is the total income?

____

2. How much is spent on food?

____

3. How much goes into savings?

____

4. What is the total rent?

____

Exercise 7- Read the Savings and Credit Statement before answering the questions.

Savings and Credit Statement (TM Bank Corp)

Transactions	Amount
Deposit	$500
Withdrawal	$100
Credit Card Fee	$25
Balance	$3,000

Comprehension Questions:

1. How much was deposited?

____

2. What is the credit card fee?

____

3. What is the balance after transactions?

____

4. How much was withdrawn?

____

Exercise 8- Read the paystub before answering the questions.

Paystub (BCX College):

Item	Amount
Gross Pay	$1,200
Deductions	$200
Net Pay	$1,000
Pay Period	Bi-weekly

Comprehension Questions:

1. What is the gross pay?

____

2. How much are the deductions?

____

3. What is the net pay?

____

4. How often is the pay period?

____

Exercise 9- Fill in the blanks with the correct words (*rent, budget, income, savings, expenses*).

1. My _______ is the money I earn from my job.

2. I pay my _______ every month to live in my apartment.

3. It is important to keep a _______ to know how much I spend.

4. _______ are things I buy or bills I pay.

5. I put money in _______ to use in the future.

Exercise 10- Complete the sentences with your personal information.

1. My name is _____________.

2. I work at a _____________.

3. I make _____________ every week.

4. I pay _____________ in rent each month.

5. I save _____________ each week.

Exercise 11- Dictation

Your teacher will read some of the new words from Exercise 2. Write down what you hear.

____

____

ANSWER KEYS

Exercise 2- Vocabulary Matching:

1. Budget - A record of income and expenses
2. Rent - Money paid regularly to live in a house or apartment
3. Savings - Money set aside for future use
4. Expenses - Money spent on things or bills
5. Income - Money earned from work or business

Exercise 3- Text 1:

1. He is looking at his tax papers.
2. He calculates his income.
3. He writes down his expenses.
4. His plan is to save money.

Exercise 4- Text 2:

1. Maria has a wallet with cards.
2. She carries debit and credit cards.
3. She pays her rent.
4. She saves some money.

Exercise 5- Rent Bill

1. $1,200 is the amount.
2. The rent is due on the 1st of every month.
3. Yes, the fee is $50.
4. ApartmentEx Company sends the bill.

Exercise 6- Household Budget Table:

1. The income is $2,500.
2. $400 is spent on food.
3. $300 goes into savings.
4. The total rent is $1,000.

Exercise 7- Savings and Credit Statement:

1. $500 was deposited.
2. The fee was $25.
3. The balance was $3000.
4. The amount withdrawn was $100.

Exercise 8- Paystub (BCX College):

1. The gross pay is $1,200.
2. The deductions are $200.
3. The net pay is $1000.
4. The pay period is bi-weekly.

Exercise 9- Fill-in-the-Blanks:

1. income
2. rent
3. budget
4. Expenses
5. savings

REFLECTION ON LEARNING

Answer the following questions and discuss your responses with your teacher or classmates.

1. What reading strategies did you learn or practice in this unit?

2. What new words did you learn?

3. What reading challenges did you face?

4. What reading strategies do you need to improve?

5. What do you want your teacher to know?

Lesson 1: Transportation and Travel

Objectives:

1. Students will read short texts and answer questions about different types of transportation.
2. Students will be able to use new words to complete sentences about different types of transportation.

Exercise 1- What do you see in the pictures?

Exercise 2- Draw a line connecting each word to its meaning.

Word	Meaning
Train	A piece of paper you need to travel
Bus	A vehicle with two wheels
Ticket	A small vehicle for one family
Car	A long vehicle that travels on tracks
Bicycle	A large vehicle that carries many people

Exercise 3- Read the text below before answering the questions.

Traveling by Bus

Alex waits for the bus. The bus goes to Front Market. He has a bus ticket. He likes to travel by bus.

Comprehension Questions:

1. Where does Alex wait?

____

2. Where does the bus go?

____

3. What does Alex have?

____

4. How does Alex feel about traveling by bus?

____

Exercise 4- Read the text below before answering the questions.

The Train Station

Sara goes to the train station. She takes the train to visit her friend. The train is fast. She has fun traveling.

Comprehension Questions:

1. Where does Sara go?

____

2. Who does Sara visit?

____

3. How is the train?

____

4. Does Sara enjoy traveling by train?

____

Exercise 5- Read the text below before answering the questions.

Driving to Work

John drives his car to work. He has a red car. It is a sunny day. He listens to music while driving.

Comprehension Questions:

1. Where does John drive?

____

2. What color is John's car?

____

3. What does John do while driving?

____

4. How is the weather when John drives?

____

Exercise 6- Read the transportation board before answering the questions.

Transportation from Miami to NYC

Transportation	Cost	Time
Bus	$50	20 hours
Train	$80	15 hours
Airplane	$150	3 hours
Car (Rental)	$100	18 hours

Comprehension Questions:

1. What is the fastest way to travel to NYC?

____

2. How much does it cost to take the bus?

____

3. How long does it take by train?

____

4. What is the cheapest way to travel?

____

Plane Ticket for Alberto Gates

Passenger	Alberto Gates
Flight	AA123
Departure	Miami
Destination	New York City
Date	October 10th
Time	8:00 AM

Comprehension Questions:

1. What is Alberto's flight number?

____

2. Where is Alberto going?

____

3. When is his flight?

____

4. What time is the flight?

____

Flight Information (LAX to Minnesota and Mississippi)

Destination	Flight Number	Departure Time
Minnesota	DL321	7:00 AM
Mississippi	UA450	9:00 AM
Minnesota	AA567	11:00 AM

Comprehension Questions:

1. What time is the flight to Mississippi?

____

2. How many flights go to Minnesota?

____

3. Which airline has the 11:00 AM flight?

____

4. What is the flight number for the 7:00 AM flight?

____

Advertisement for Scooter and Bike in DC

Vehicle	Price per Hour	Rental Location
Scooter	$5	Near the Metro Station
Bike	$3	Downtown Park

Comprehension Questions:

1. How much does it cost to rent a scooter?

____

2. Where can you rent a bike?

____

3. Which vehicle is cheaper to rent per hour?

____

4. Where can you rent a scooter?

____

1. I wait at the _______ stop every morning. (bus)

2. I buy a _______ to take the train. (ticket)

3. He rides his _______ to the park. (bicycle)

4. The _______ is a fast way to travel. (train)

5. She drives her _______ to school. (car)

Exercise 11- Complete the sentences with words you learned in this lesson.

1. She needs a _______ to get on the airplane.

2. The _______ goes on the tracks.

3. He rents a _______ to ride around the park.

4. I like to take the _______ to the city center.

5. The _______ is a good way to travel with family.

Exercise 12- Dictation

Your teacher will read some of the new words from Exercise 2. Write down what you hear.

____

____

ANSWER KEYS

Exercise 2- Vocabulary Matching:

1. Train - A long vehicle that travels on tracks
2. Bus - A large vehicle that carries many people
3. Ticket - A piece of paper you need to travel
4. Car - A small vehicle for one family
5. Bicycle - A vehicle with two wheels

Exercise 3- Text 1:

1. He waits at the bus stop.
2. It goes to Front Market.
3. He has a bus ticket.
4. He likes it.

Exercise 4- Text 2:

1. Sara goes to the train station.
2. She visits her friend.
3. The train is fast.
4. Yes, she has fun.

Exercise 5- Text 3:

1. John drives to work.
2. His car is red.
3. He listens to music.
4. It is sunny.

Exercise 6- Transportation Board:

1. The airplane is the fastest way.
2. It costs $50.
3. It takes 15 hours by train.
4. The bus is the cheapest way to travel.

Exercise 7- Plane Ticket:

1. Alberto's flight number is AA123.
2. He is going to New York City.
3. His flight is on October 10th.
4. His flight is at 8:00 AM.

Exercise 8- Flight Information Board:

1. The flight is at 9:00 AM.
2. Two flights go to Minnesota.
3. AA (American Airlines has the 11:00 AM flight.
4. DL321 is the flight number.

Exercise 9- Advertisement:

1. It costs $5 per hour.
2. You can rent a bike at Downtown Park.
3. Renting a bike is cheaper.
4. You can rent a scooter near the Metro Station.

Exercise 10- Fill-in-the-Blanks:

1. bus
2. ticket
3. bicycle
4. train
5. car

Exercise 11- Complete the Sentences:

1. ticket
2. train
3. bicycle
4. bus
5. car

Lesson 2: Time and Weather

Objectives:

1. Students will read short texts and answer questions about time and weather.
2. Students will use new words to complete sentences about weather and time in real-life situations.

Exercise 1- What do you see in the pictures?

Exercise 2- Draw a line connecting each word to its meaning.

Word	Meaning
Morning	When water falls from the sky
Rainy	The time of day when the sun rises
Cloudy	The time when the sky is dark
Night	The time of day before it gets dark
Evening	When there are many clouds in the sky

Exercise 3- Read the text below before answering the questions.

Morning Time

Luis wakes up in the morning. It is sunny outside. He drinks his coffee. The weather is warm. He feels great.

Comprehension Questions:

1. What time of day is it?

____

2. What is the weather like?

____

3. What does Luis drink?

____

4. How does Luis feel about the morning?

____

A Cloudy Afternoon

Maria goes for a walk in the afternoon. The sky is cloudy. She wears a light jacket. She enjoys her walk.

Comprehension Questions:

1. When does Maria go for a walk?

____

2. What is the weather like?

____

3. What does Maria wear?

____

4. Does Maria enjoy her walk?

____

A Rainy Evening

Ahmed sees it is rainy in the evening. He stays inside his house. He watches TV. He waits for the rain to stop.

Comprehension Questions:

1. When does Ahmed see the rain?

____

2. What does Ahmed do at home?

____

3. What is the weather like?

____

4. Why does Ahmed stay inside?

____

5-Day Weather Forecast (Miami)

Day	Weather	Temperature
Monday	Sunny	80°F
Tuesday	Rainy	75°F
Wednesday	Cloudy	78°F
Thursday	Windy	79°F
Friday	Hot	85°F

Comprehension Questions:

1. What is the weather on Monday?

____

2. What is the temperature on Wednesday?

____

3. What day is rainy?

____

4. Which day is the hottest?

____

Time in Major Cities Board:

City	Time
Los Angeles	9:00 AM
Dallas	11:00 AM
Philadelphia	12:00 PM

Comprehension Questions:

1. What is the time in Los Angeles?

____

2. Which city is one hour ahead of Dallas?

____

3. What is the time difference between Los Angeles and Philadelphia?

____

4. What time is it in Dallas?

____

Class Schedule at BG Community College (Mississippi)

Class	Day	Time
Math	Monday	9:00 AM
English	Tuesday	10:00 AM
Computer Skills	Wednesday	1:00 PM
History	Thursday	11:00 AM
Science	Friday	2:00 PM

Comprehension Questions:

1. When is the Math class?

____

2. What day is the Computer Skills class?

____

3. What class is at 11:00 AM?

____

4. Which class is on Friday?

____

Bad Weather Warning (Oklahoma City)

Attention: There is a storm coming to Oklahoma City. It will be very windy. Please stay inside. Stay safe and be careful.

Comprehension Questions:

1. What type of weather is coming to Oklahoma City?

____

2. What should people do during the storm?

____

3. Why should people stay inside?

____

4. How does the announcement ask people to be?

____

1. In the _______, the sun rises.

2. It is _______ when the sky has many clouds.

3. When water falls from the sky, it is _______.

4. The weather is very _______ today. It is 90°F.

5. In the _______, it starts to get dark.

Exercise 11- Complete the sentences with words you learned in this lesson.

1. I wear a jacket when it is _______ outside.

2. I need an umbrella because it is _______.

3. The sun sets in the _______.

4. I wake up early in the _______.

5. The weather is _______; it is 85°F today.

Exercise 12- Dictation

Your teacher will read some of the new words from Exercise 2. Write down what you hear.

____

____

ANSWER KEYS

Exercise 2- Vocabulary Matching:
1. Morning - The time of day when the sun rises
2. Rainy - When water falls from the sky
3. Cloudy - When there are many clouds in the sky
4. Night - The time when the sky is dark
5. Evening - The time of day before it gets dark

Exercise 3- Text 1:
1. It is the morning time.
2. It is sunny.
3. He drinks coffee.
4. He feels great.

Exercise 4- Text 2:
1. She goes in the afternoon.
2. It is cloudy.
3. She wears a light jacket.
4. Yes, she enjoys it.

Exercise 5- Text 3:
1. Ahmed sees the rain in the evening.
2. He watches TV.
3. The weather is rainy.
4. He stays inside because it is raining.

Exercise 6- Weather Forecast:
1. The weather is sunny.
2. The temperature is 78°F.
3. Tuesday is rainy.
4. Friday is the hottest at 85°F.

Exercise 7- Time in Major Cities Board:
1. The time is 9:00 AM.
2. Philadelphia is one hour ahead.
3. The time difference is 3 hours.
4. It is 11:00 AM.

Exercise 8- Class Schedule:
1. It is on Monday at 9:00 AM.
2. It is on Wednesday.
3. History is at 11:00 AM.
4. Science is on Friday.

Exercise 9- Weather Warning:
1. A storm is coming.
2. People should stay inside.
3. They should stay inside because it will be very windy.
4. It asks people to be safe and careful.

Exercise 10- Fill-in-the-Blanks:
1. morning
2. cloudy
3. rainy
4. hot
5. evening

Exercise 11- Complete the Sentences:
1. cold
2. rainy
3. evening
4. morning
5. hot

Lesson 3: Community Agencies and Services

Objectives:

1. Students will be able to read short texts and answer questions about community agencies and services.
2. Students will use new words to complete sentences about community agencies and services.

Exercise 1- What do you see in the pictures?

Exercise 2- Draw a line connecting each word to its meaning.

Word	Meaning
Library	A service that helps keep people safe
Police	A place to stay if someone does not have a home
Clinic	A place to get free food
Shelter	A place to read and borrow books
Food Bank	A place where people go to see a doctor

Exercise 3- Read the text below before answering the questions.

The Library

Anna likes to learn. She goes to the library. She reads books about health. The library is free.

Comprehension Questions:

1. Where does Anna go?

____

2. What does Anna read about?

____

3. How much does the library cost?

____

4. Why does Anna go to the library?

____

Exercise 4- Read the text below before answering the questions.

The Police Station

David visits the police station. He asks for help to find his lost bike. The police are friendly. They promise to help him.

Comprehension Questions:

1. Where does David go?

____

2. What does David ask for?

____

3. How are the police?

____

4. What do the police promise to do?

____

Exercise 5- Read the text below before answering the questions.

The Community Clinic

Sara goes to the clinic. She sees a doctor for her cough. The doctor gives her medicine. Sara feels better.

Comprehension Questions:

1. Where does Sara go?

____

2. Why does she visit the place?

____

3. Who helps Sara?

____

4. How does Sara feel after the visit?

____

Community Agencies and Services Information

Agency/Service	Location	Hours
Food Bank	123 Main Street	Mon-Fri, 9 AM - 5 PM
Public Library	456 Elm Avenue	Mon-Sat, 10 AM - 6 PM
Community Clinic	789 Oak Road	Mon-Fri, 8 AM - 4 PM

Comprehension Questions:

1. Where is the food bank located?

____

2. What are the library's hours?

____

3. What service is on Oak Road?

____

4. Which agency is open on Saturday?

____

Housing Information

Housing Service	Details
City Shelter	Offers a place to sleep and eat
Rent Assistance	Helps pay rent for families
Low-Income Housing	Provides affordable apartments

Comprehension Questions:

1. What kind of information does the table show?

____

2. What does the City Shelter offer?

____

3. Who does Rent Assistance help?

____

4. What type of apartments does Low-Income Housing provide?

____

Exercise 8- Read the social services information below before answering the questions.

Social Services Information

Service	Details
Food Assistance	Helps families get food
Job Training	Teaches people new skills for work
Childcare Support	Helps pay for the care of young children

Comprehension Questions:

1. What does Food Assistance help with?

____

2. Who can benefit from Job Training?

____

3. What support is given for young children?

____

4. Which service helps with learning skills for work?

____

Free Adult Education Classes Information

Class	Day/Time	Location
ESL	Mon/Wed, 6 PM	Community Center
GED Prep	Tue/Thu, 7 PM	Learning Center
HiSET Prep	Sat, 9 AM	Adult School

Comprehension Questions:

1. When is the ESL class?

____

2. What class is on Saturday?

____

3. Where are the GED prep classes held?

____

4. What time does the HiSET class start?

____

1. I go to the _______ to borrow books.

2. The _______ helps keep the city safe.

3. If I am sick, I go to the _______.

4. People without homes can stay at the _______.

5. A _______ gives food to people who need it.

1. Families can get free meals at the _______.

2. When I have a cold, I visit the _______.

3. The _______ are friendly and helpful when I need help.

4. A _______ is a safe place for those without a home.

5. I can find free books at the ______.

Exercise 12- Dictation

Your teacher will read some of the new words from Exercise 2. Write down what you hear.

____

____

ANSWER KEYS

Exercise 2- Vocabulary Matching:

1. Library - A place to read and borrow books
2. Police - A service that helps keep people safe
3. Clinic - A place where people go to see a doctor
4. Shelter - A place to stay if someone does not have a home
5. Food Bank - A place to get free food

Exercise 3- Text 1:

1. She goes to the library.
2. She reads about health.
3. The library is free.
4. She likes to learn.

Exercise 4- Text 2:

1. David goes to the police station.
2. He asks for help to find his lost bike.
3. They are friendly.
4. They promise to help him.

Exercise 5- Text 3:

1. She goes to the clinic.
2. She has a cough.
3. A doctor helps her.
4. She feels better.

Exercise 6- Community Agencies and Services Information:

1. It is at 123 Main Street.
2. The library is open Monday to Saturday, from 10 AM to 6 PM.
3. The community clinic is on Oak Road.
4. The public library is open.

Exercise 7- Housing Information:

1. The table shows housing information.
2. It offers a place to sleep and eat.
3. It helps pay rent for families.
4. It provides affordable apartments.

Exercise 8- Social Services Information:

1. It helps families get food.
2. People who want to learn new work skills can benefit.
3. Childcare support is given to young children.
4. Job training helps with learning skills for work.

Exercise 9- Free Adult Education Classes Information:

1. The ESL class is on Monday and Wednesday at 6 PM.
2. The HiSET class is on Saturday.
3. The prep classes are held at the Learning Center.
4. It starts at 9 AM.

Exercise 10- Fill-in-the-Blanks:

1. library
2. police
3. clinic
4. shelter
5. food bank

Exercise 11- Complete the Sentences:

1. food bank
2. clinic
3. police
4. shelter
5. library

REFLECTION ON LEARNING

Answer the following questions and discuss your responses with your teacher or classmates.

1. What reading strategies did you learn or practice in this unit?

2. What new words did you learn?

3. What reading challenges did you face?

4. What reading strategies do you need to improve?

5. What do you want your teacher to know?

Lesson 1: Accessing Health Care

Objectives:

1. Students will read short texts and answer questions about visiting a doctor, getting insurance, and using pharmacies.
2. Students will use new words to complete sentences about accessing and using the health care system.

Exercise 1- What do you see in the pictures?

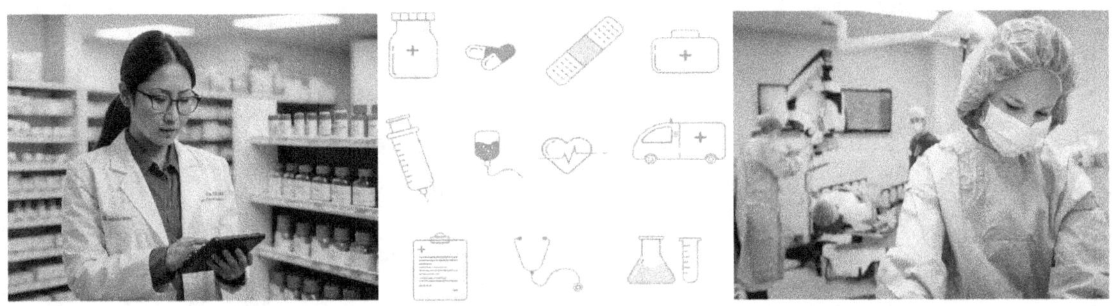

Exercise 2- Draw a line connecting each word to its meaning.

Word	Meaning
Doctor	A plan that helps pay for health care
Clinic	A person who helps sick people
Insurance	A place where you buy medicine
Prescription	A place to see a doctor
Pharmacy	A paper from the doctor to get medicine

Exercise 3- Read the text below before answering the questions.

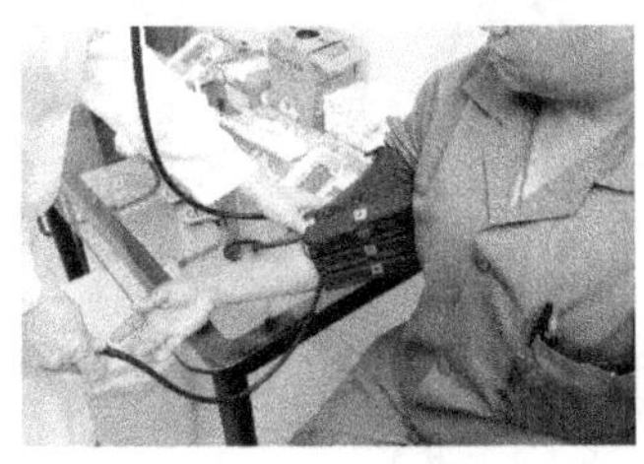

Visiting a Clinic

Maria visits a clinic. She is not feeling well. The doctor talks to her. He gives her medicine to take.

Comprehension Questions:

1. Where does Maria go?

2. Why does Maria go there?

3. Who talks to Maria?

4. What does the doctor give to Maria?

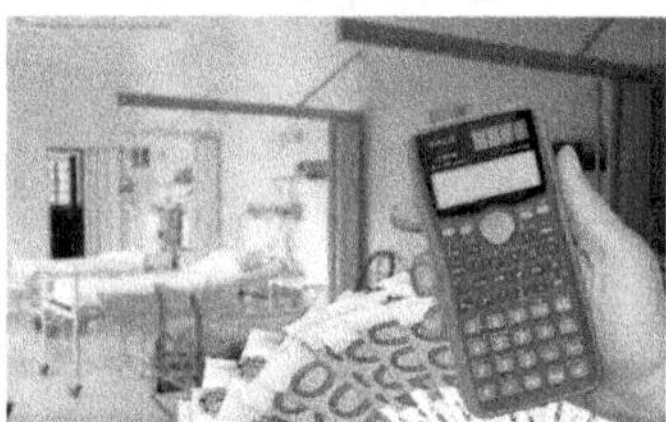

Medical Insurance

John uses his insurance card. He goes to the hospital. The insurance helps pay for his care. He is happy to have it.

Comprehension Questions:

1. What does John use at the hospital?

2. Where does John go?

3. What does the insurance help pay for?

4. How does John feel about having insurance?

The Pharmacy

Avion goes to the pharmacy. She gives the pharmacist her prescription. He finds the right medicine for her. She buys the medicine.

Comprehension Questions:

1. Where does Avion go?

____

2. Who takes Avion's prescription?

____

3. What does the pharmacist find?

____

4. What does Avion do with the medicine?

____

Exercise 6- Read the insurance options below before answering the questions.

Medical Insurance Options and Costs

Plan	Coverage	Cost per Month
Basic Plan	Doctor visits only	$50
Standard Plan	Doctor visits + Hospital Stay	$100
Premium Plan	All health care needs	$200

Comprehension Questions:

1. What does the Basic Plan cover?

____

2. Which plan costs $100 per month?

____

3. What plan covers all health care needs?

____

4. How much is the Premium Plan?

____

Information: Doctors and Specialists

Type of Doctor	What They Do
General Doctor	Helps with common health issues
Dentist	Takes care of teeth
Eye Doctor	Checks eyes and vision
Pediatrician	Helps children
Cardiologist	Checks heart health

Comprehension Questions:

1. Who takes care of teeth?

____

2. What does a general doctor do?

____

3. Who helps children?

____

4. Which doctor checks the heart?

____

Urgent Care Clinic Information

Clinic	Location	Hours
Quick Care	Main Street	8 AM - 8 PM
Health Now	2nd Avenue	9 AM - 9 PM
City Clinic	Park Road	7 AM - 10 PM

Comprehension Questions:

1. Which clinic is on Main Street?

____

2. What are the hours for City Clinic?

____

3. What time does Health Now open?

____

4. Which clinic is open the longest?

____

Drugstore Information

Drugstore	Services	Hours
HealthPlus	Medicine, Vaccines	9 AM - 8 PM
WellnessPharm	Medicine, Health Advice	8 AM - 7 PM
FamilyPharmacy	Medicine, Vitamins	7 AM - 9 PM

Comprehension Questions:

1. Which drugstore offers vaccines?

____

2. What time does FamilyPharmacy open?

____

3. Which store provides health advice?

____

4. What are the hours for WellnessPharm?

____

1. I go to the _______ when I need medicine.

2. My _______ plan helps me pay for health care.

3. The _______ gives me a prescription for my cough.

4. The _______ is open late for sick people.

5. I need a _______ to get my medicine.

Exercise 11- Complete the sentences with words you learned in this lesson.

1. I need to visit the _______ for my eye check-up.

2. The _______ helps me find the right medicine.

3. A _______ helps me when I am sick.

4. I use my _______ to help pay for my doctor's visit.

5. The doctor gives me a _______ to get my medicine.

Exercise 12- Dictation

Your teacher will read some of the new words from Exercise 2. Write down what you hear.

____

____

ANSWER KEYS

Exercise 2- Vocabulary Matching:
1. Doctor - A person who helps sick people
2. Clinic - A place to see a doctor
3. Insurance - A plan that helps pay for health care
4. Prescription - A paper from the doctor to get medicine
5. Pharmacy - A place where you buy medicine

Exercise 3- Text 1:
1. She goes to a clinic.
2. She is not feeling well.
3. A doctor talks to Maria.
4. The doctor gives her medicine.

Exercise 4- Text 2:
1. John uses his insurance card.
2. He goes to the hospital.
3. It helps pay for his health care costs.
4. He feels happy.

Exercise 5- Text 3:
1. She goes to the pharmacy.
2. The pharmacist takes her prescription.
3. The pharmacist finds the right medicine.
4. She buys it.

Exercise 6- Medical Insurance Options:
1. It covers doctor visits only.
2. The Standard Plan costs $100 per month.
3. The Premium Plan covers all this.
4. It costs $200.

Exercise 7- Doctors and Specialists:
1. The dentist takes care of teeth.
2. A general doctor helps with common health issues.
3. A pediatrician helps children.
4. A cardiologist checks the heart.

Exercise 8- Clinic Information:
1. Quick Care is on Main Street.
2. City Clinic opens from 7 AM to 10 PM.
3. Health Now opens at 9 AM.
4. City Clinic is open the longest.

Exercise 9- Drugstore Information:
1. HealthPlus offers vaccines.
2. It opens at 7 AM.
3. WellnessPharm provides this.
4. It opens from 8 AM to 7 PM.

Exercise 10- Fill-in-the-Blanks:
1. pharmacy
2. insurance
3. doctor
4. clinic
5. prescription

Exercise 11- Complete the Sentences:
1. eye doctor
2. pharmacist
3. doctor
4. insurance
5. prescription

Lesson 2: Medical Information and Forms

Objectives:

1. Students will read short texts and answer questions about completing forms in health care.
2. Students will use new words to complete sentences about the simple forms used in health care situations.

Exercise 1- What do you see in the picture?

Exercise 2- Draw a line connecting each word to its meaning.

Word	Meaning
Patient	The day someone was born
Appointment	A person's name written on a form
Signature	A person who works at the front desk of a doctor's office or hospital
Receptionist	A set time to see a doctor or dentist
Date of Birth	A person who sees a doctor

Exercise 3- Read the text below before answering the questions.

Signing a Health Form

Matthew fills out a health form. He writes his name and address. He signs his name at the bottom of the form. The form is for a clinic visit.

Comprehension Questions:

1. What does Matthew fill out?

____

2. What does he write on the form?

____

3. Where does he sign his name?

____

4. What is the form for?

____

Exercise 4- Read the text below before answering the questions.

Doctor's Appointment

Carlos calls to make an appointment. He talks to the nurse. She asks for his date of birth. Carlos writes down the appointment time.

Comprehension Questions:

1. What does Carlos call to do?

____

2. Who speaks with him?

____

3. What information does the nurse ask for?

____

4. What does Carlos write down?

____

Exercise 5- Read the text below before answering the questions.

Insurance Card

Ana shows her insurance card. She gives it to the receptionist. The receptionist checks the card. Ana waits to see the doctor.

Comprehension Questions:

1. What does Ana show?

____

2. Who does she give the card to?

____

3. What does the receptionist do with the card?

____

4. What does Ana do after showing the card?

____

Exercise 6- Read the exam form below before answering the questions.

Dental Exam Form for Amari Joseph

Field	Information
Name	Amari Joseph
Date of Birth	01/15/1990
Appointment Date	11/05/2024
Dentist	Dr. Lee
Reason for Visit	Regular check-up

Comprehension Questions:

1. Who is the form for?

____

2. When is Amari's date of birth?

____

3. What is the reason for the visit?

____

4. Who is the dentist?

____

Physical Medical Form for Kim Soyoun

Field	Information
Name	Kim Soyoun
Date of Birth	04/12/1985
Doctor	Dr. Smith
Visit Date	12/01/2024
Purpose	Physical exam

Comprehension Questions:

1. What is the name on the form?

____

2. What is the purpose of the visit?

____

3. When is the visit date?

____

4. Who will Kim see?

____

Health Insurance Card for Pablo Esteban

Field	Details
Name	Pablo Esteban
Insurance Company	HealthFirst
Policy Number	1353789
Effective Date	01/01/2024
Coverage	Medical and Dental

Comprehension Questions:

1. What is the name on the card?

____

2. What is the insurance company?

____

3. What type of coverage does the card provide?

____

4. What is the effective date of the policy?

____

Exercise 9- Read the appointment reminder below before answering the questions.

Appointment Reminder Card for Kelly Mamadou

Field	Details
Name	Kelly Mamadou
Appointment Date	11/10/2024
Time	10:00 AM
Location	Green Health Clinic

Comprehension Questions:

1. Who is the reminder for?

____

2. What time is the appointment?

____

3. Where is the appointment?

____

4. What is the appointment date?

____

Exercise 10- Fill in the blanks with the correct words *(appointment, insurance, signature, date of birth, patient).*

1. I need to include my _______ on the health form.

2. My _______ is set for 3:00 PM tomorrow.

3. The _______ helps pay for my doctor visit.

4. I am the _______ seeing the doctor.

5. My _______ is 05/25/1992.

Exercise 11- Complete the sentences with words you learned in this lesson.

1. The _______ checks the insurance card.

2. _______ helps pay for medical bills.

3. The nurse writes my name on the _______.

4. I make an _______ to see my doctor.

5. The _______ signs the form before the visit.

Exercise 12- Dictation

Your teacher will read some of the new words from Exercise 2. Write down what you hear.

____

____

ANSWER KEYS

Exercise 2- Vocabulary Matching:

1. Patient - A person who sees a doctor
2. Appointment - A set time to see a doctor or dentist
3. Signature - A person's name written on a form
4. Receptionist - A person who works at the front desk of a doctor's office or hospital
5. Date of Birth - The day someone was born

Exercise 3- Text 1:

1. He fills out a health form.
2. He writes his name and address.
3. He signs his name at the bottom of the form.
4. The form is for a clinic visit.

Exercise 4- Text 2:

1. He calls to make an appointment.
2. A nurse speaks with him.
3. She asks for his date of birth.
4. He writes down the appointment time.

Exercise 5- Text 3:

1. Ana shows her insurance card.
2. She gives the card to the receptionist.
3. The receptionist checks the card.
4. She waits to see the doctor.

Exercise 6- Dental Exam Form:

1. The form is for Amari Joseph.
2. Amari's date of birth was on January 15th, 1990.

3. The purpose is for a regular check-up.
4. Dr. Lee is the dentist.

Exercise 7- Physical Medical Form:

1. Kim Soyoun is the name on the form.
2. A physical exam is the purpose.
3. The visit is on December 1st, 2024.
4. She will see Dr. Smith.

Exercise 8- Health Insurance Card:

1. Pablo Esteban is the name on the card.
2. The insurance company is HealthFirst.
3. The card provides medical and dental coverage.
4. It is effective from January 1st, 2024.

Exercise 9- Appointment Reminder Card:

1. The reminder is for Kelly Mamadou.
2. The appointment is at 10:00 AM.
3. The appointment is at Green Health Clinic.
4. The appointment is on November 10th, 2024.

Exercise 10- Fill-in-the-Blanks:

1. signature
2. appointment
3. insurance
4. patient
5. date of birth

Exercise 11- Complete the Sentences:

1. receptionist
2. health insurance
3. form
4. appointment
5. patient

Lesson 3: Health Care and Prevention

Objectives:

1. Students will read short texts and answer questions about health care and prevention.
2. Students will use new words to complete sentences about staying healthy and preventing sickness.

Exercise 1- What do you see in the pictures?

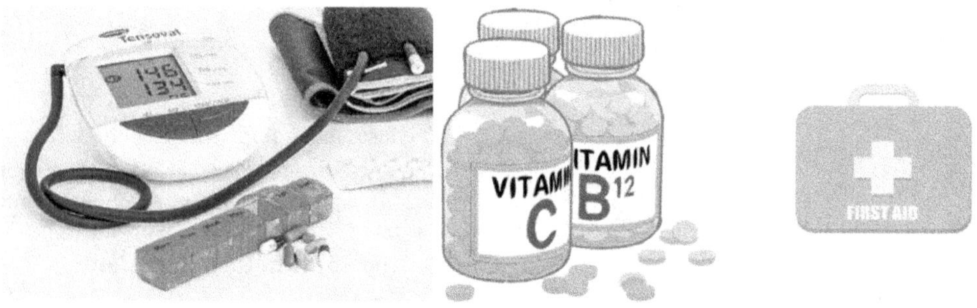

Exercise 2- Draw a line connecting each word to its meaning.

Word	Meaning
Exercise	The food that you eat
Diet	To move your body to stay strong and healthy
Vaccine	Keeping clean to stay healthy
Wash	A shot to prevent sickness
Hygiene	To clean your body

Exercise 3- Read the text below before answering the questions.

Going for a Walk

Leo walks every morning. He likes to exercise. Walking helps him feel good. He wears his sneakers.

Comprehension Questions:

1. What does Leo do every morning?

____

2. How does walking help Leo?

____

3. What does Leo wear when walking?

____

4. Why does Leo walk?

____

Eating Healthy Food

Sara eats fruits and vegetables. She drinks water with her meals. She wants to stay healthy. She does not eat too much sugar.

Comprehension Questions:

1. What does Sara eat?

____

2. What does she drink with her meals?

____

3. Why does she eat foods like this?

____

4. What does she avoid eating?

____

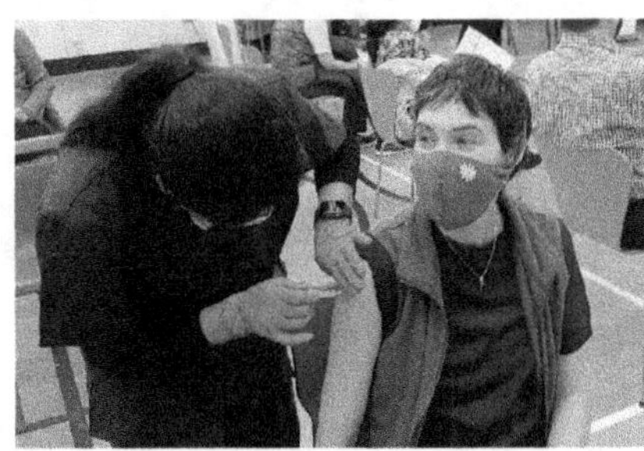

Getting a Flu Shot

Anna goes to the clinic. She gets a flu shot. The nurse gives her the shot. The shot helps Anna stay healthy.

Comprehension Questions:

1. Where does Anna go?

____

2. What does Anna get?

____

3. Who gives it to Anna?

____

4. How does the shot help Anna?

____

Exercise 6- Read the tips below before answering the questions.

Healthy Eating Tips

Tip	Description
Eat breakfast.	Start your day with healthy foods.
Drink water.	Drink 8 cups of water every day.
Eat fruits & veggies.	Add more fruits and vegetables to your meals.
Limit sugar.	Eat less candy, soda, and sweet foods.
Balanced meals.	Have a mix of protein, carbs, and veggies.

Comprehension Questions:

1. How many cups of water should you drink every day?

____

2. What kind of food should you limit?

____

3. What should be eaten for breakfast?

____

4. What should be included in a balanced meal?

____

Free Class Schedule at Valley Community Center

Class	Day/Time	Details
Yoga	Monday, 6 PM	Stretch and relax
Zumba	Wednesday, 7 PM	Dance to stay active
Nutrition Class	Friday, 5 PM	Learn about healthy food

Comprehension Questions:

1. What day is the yoga class?

____

2. What is zumba good for?

____

3. When is the nutrition class?

____

4. What can you learn about in the nutrition class?

____

Free Flu Shots Information

Location	Day/Time	Details
Community Clinic	Tuesday, 9 AM - 12 PM	Free flu shots for everyone
Local Pharmacy	Thursday, 1 PM - 4 PM	Show identification for free COVID shots

Comprehension Questions:

1. Where can you go on Tuesday for a flu shot?

____

2. What time are flu shots available at the pharmacy?

____

3. Who can get a free flu shot at the community clinic?

____

4. What should you do to get a shot at the local pharmacy?

____

Healthy Habits and Hygiene

Habit	How It Helps
Wash hands.	Keeps germs away.
Sleep well.	Gives your body rest and energy.
Exercise often.	Makes your body strong.
Eat healthy.	Helps you feel good.
Brush your teeth.	Keeps your teeth clean and strong.

Comprehension Questions:

1. How does washing your hands help you?

____

2. Why is sleeping well important?

____

3. What does eating healthy do for you?

____

4. How does brushing your teeth help?

____

1. I drink water every day to stay _______.

2. I wash my hands to keep away _______.

3. A _______ helps me feel better when I am sick.

4. I like to _______ in the park every evening.

5. I get a _______ to prevent the flu.

Exercise 11- Complete the sentences with words you learned in this lesson.

1. To stay strong, I need to _______ every morning.

2. A _______ helps keep my body safe from sickness.

3. I eat a balanced _______ to stay fit.

4. The _______ gives me medicine when I am sick.

5. I _______ my hands after using the bathroom.

Exercise 12- Dictation

Your teacher will read some of the new words from Exercise 2. Write down what you hear.

____

____

ANSWER KEYS

Exercise 2- Vocabulary Matching:
1. Exercise - To move your body to stay strong and healthy
2. Diet - The food that you eat
3. Vaccine - A shot to prevent sickness
4. Wash - To clean your body
5. Hygiene – Keeping clean to stay healthy

Exercise 3- Text 1:
1. Leo walks every morning.
2. Walking helps him feel good.
3. Leo wears sneakers.
4. He walks as a form of exercise.

Exercise 4- Text 2:
1. Sara eats fruits and vegetables.
2. She drinks water.
3. She does this to stay healthy.
4. She avoids eating too much sugar.

Exercise 5- Text 3:
1. She goes to the clinic.
2. She gets the flu shot.
3. The nurse gives it to her.
4. It helps her stay healthy.

Exercise 6- Healthy Eating Tips:
1. You should drink 8 cups of water.
2. You should limit candy, soda, and sweet foods.
3. Healthy foods should be eaten for breakfast.
4. A balanced meal has protein, carbs, and veggies.

Exercise 7- Free Class Schedule:
1. The yoga class is on Monday.
2. Zumba is good for staying active.
3. The nutrition class is on Friday at 5 PM.
4. You can learn about healthy food.

Exercise 8- Free Flu Shots Information:
1. You can go to the community clinic.
2. They are available from 1 PM to 4 PM.
3. Everyone can get a flu shot.
4. You must show identification.

Exercise 9- Healthy Habits and Hygiene Board:
1. It keeps germs away.
2. It gives your body rest and energy.
3. It helps you feel good.
4. It keeps your teeth clean and strong.

Exercise 10- Fill-in-the-Blanks:
1. healthy
2. germs
3. doctor
4. exercise
5. vaccine

Exercise 11- Complete the Sentences:
1. exercise
2. vaccine
3. diet
4. doctor
5. wash

REFLECTION ON LEARNING

Answer the following questions and discuss your responses with your teacher or classmates.

1. What reading strategies did you learn or practice in this unit?

2. What new words did you learn?

3. What reading challenges did you face?

4. What reading strategies do you need to improve?

5. What do you want your teacher to know?

Lesson 1: Job Searching

Objectives:

1. Students will read short texts and answer questions about job searching and interviewing.
2. Students will use new words to complete sentences about finding a job and preparing for an interview.

Exercise 1- What do you see in the pictures?

Exercise 2- Draw a line connecting each word to its meaning.

Words	Meanings
Resume	Extra things you get from a job, like health insurance or vacation
Interview	A paper with your work and skills
Apply	The money you earn from working
Salary	A meeting to talk about a job
Benefits	To ask for a job

Exercise 3- Read the text below before answering the questions.

Job Searching Online

Emily is looking for a job online. She finds many job ads. She wants to work in a store. She applies for two jobs.

Comprehension Questions:

1. What is Emily looking for online?

____

2. How many jobs does she apply for?

____

3. Where does Emily want to work?

____

4. What does Emily find online?

____

Exercise 4- Read the text below before answering the questions.

Preparing for an Interview

Carlos has an interview tomorrow. He is nervous. He picks out his best clothes. He practices answering questions. He wants to be ready.

Comprehension Questions:

1. What is Carlos preparing for?

____

2. What does he pick out?

____

3. What does he practice?

____

4. How does he feel about the interview?

____

A Job Interview

Aisha goes to her interview. She arrives early. She smiles and shakes hands. Aisha answers questions about her skills.

Comprehension Questions:

1. Where does Aisha go?

____

2. What does she do when she arrives?

____

3. What does Aisha talk about in the interview?

____

4. How does Aisha act during the interview?

____

Job Ads with Benefits

Job	Location	Salary	Benefits
Cashier	Grocery Store	$15 per hour	Health insurance
Office Clerk	Small Business	$17 per hour	Paid vacation

Comprehension Questions:

1. Where is the cashier job located?

____

2. How much is the office clerk's salary?

____

3. Which job offers paid vacation?

____

4. What benefit does the cashier job offer?

____

Tips for Online Job Searching

Tip	Description
Use job websites.	Search for jobs on sites like Indeed or LinkedIn.
Check every day.	Look for new jobs daily.
Apply for many jobs.	Send applications to more than one job.

Comprehension Questions:

1. Where should you search for jobs?

____

2. How often should you check for jobs?

____

3. Why should you apply for many jobs?

____

4. What websites can you use for job searching?

____

Tips on Preparing for Job Interviews:

Tip	Details
Dress nicely.	Wear clean and professional clothes.
Practice questions.	Practice answering common interview questions.
Be on time.	Arrive 10 minutes early.
Bring your resume.	Have a copy of your resume to give to the interviewer.

Comprehension Questions:

1. How should you dress for an interview?

____

2. What should you practice before the interview?

____

3. When should you arrive at the interview?

____

4. What should you bring with you to the interview?

____

Resume for Tony Adams

Tony Adams

CONTACT

124-442-7869

tony.adams@email.com

423 Maple Street,
Apt. 5B
Springfield, IL 62704

OBJECTIVE

To use my skills to help and support customers

SKILLS

- Good with people
- Has basic computer skills
- Able to use a cash register

EDUCATION

Green Valley Community College
Associate Degree in Business Administration

September 2017 – June 2019

WORK EXPERIENCE

Store Clerk
Sunnybrook Grocers
(June 2021 – August 2023)

- Helped customers find items in the store
- Worked at the cash register

Receptionist
Riverside Medical Center
(September 2019 – May 2021

- Greeted visitors
- Answered phone calls
- Helped people make appointments

Comprehension Questions:

1. What is Tony looking for?

____

2. What jobs did Tony have before?

____

3. What skill does Tony have?

____

4. What college did he attend?

____

Exercise 10- Fill in the blanks with the correct words (*apply, resume, benefits, salary, interview*).

1. I write my _______ to show my work experience.

2. I go to an _______ to talk about a job.

3. I _______ for a new job at a bank.

4. The _______ at my job is $18 per hour.

5. My job gives me health _______.

Exercise 11- Complete the sentences with words you learned in this lesson.

1. My new _______ is good; I make $20 per hour.

2. Before my _______, I practice speaking clearly.

3. I send my _______ to many companies.

4. A job with good _______ can help you with health costs.

5. When I _______ for a job, I fill out an application.

Exercise 12- Dictation

Your teacher will read some of the new words from Exercise 2. Write down what you hear.

____

____

ANSWER KEYS

Exercise 2- Vocabulary Matching:

1. Resume - A paper with your work and skills
2. Interview - A meeting to talk about a job
3. Apply - To ask for a job
4. Salary - The money you earn from working
5. Benefits - Extra things you get from a job, like health insurance or vacation

Exercise 3- Text 1:

1. Emily is looking for a job.
2. She applies for two jobs.
3. She wants to work in a store.
4. She finds many job ads.

Exercise 4- Text 2:

1. Carlos is preparing for an interview.
2. He picks out his best clothes.
3. He practices answering questions.
4. He feels nervous.

Exercise 5- Text 3:

1. Aisha goes to an interview.
2. She smiles and shakes hands.
3. She talks about her skills.
4. She is polite.

Exercise 6- Job Ad with Benefits:

1. It is located at a grocery store.
2. It is $17 per hour.
3. The office clerk offers paid vacation.
4. It offers health insurance.

Exercise 7- Tips for Online Job Searching:

1. You should search on job websites.
2. You should check every day.
3. You would have more chances to get hired.
4. You can use Indeed and LinkedIn.

Exercise 8- Tips on Preparing for Job Interviews:

1. You should dress nicely with clean and professional clothes.
2. You should practice answering common interview questions.
3. You should arrive 10 minutes early.
4. You should bring your resume.

Exercise 9- Sample Resume for Tony Adams:

1. Tony is looking for a job in customer service.
2. He worked as a store clerk and receptionist.
3. He is good with people, has basic computer skills and can use a cash register.
4. He attended Green Valley Community College.

Exercise 10- Fill-in-the-Blanks:

1. resume
2. interview
3. apply
4. salary
5. benefits

Exercise 11- Complete the Sentences:

1. salary
2. interview
3. resume
4. benefits
5. apply

Lesson 2: Wages, Benefits, Employee Rights, and Unions

Objectives:

1. Students will read short texts and answer questions about wages, benefits, and employee rights and unions.
2. Students will use new words to complete sentences about wages, benefits, employee protection and worker organizations.

Exercise 1- What do you see in the pictures?

Exercise 2- Draw a line connecting each word to its meaning.

Word	Meaning
Wages	Money earned for work
Deduction	Money taken out of your pay
Rights	Things you are allowed to do at work
Union	A group that helps protect workers
Paystub	A paper showing how much money you made

Exercise 3- Read the text below before answering the questions.

Talking About Wages

Luis works at a restaurant. He earns $14 per hour. He is happy with his wages. He wants to save money.

Comprehension Questions:

1. Where does Luis work?

---

2. How much does he earn per hour?

---

3. How does Luis feel about his wages?

---

4. What does he want to do with his money?

Exercise 4- Read the text below before answering the questions.

Job Benefits

Maria gets benefits from her job. She has health insurance. She also gets vacation days. She is thankful for her benefits.

Comprehension Questions:

1. What does Maria get from her job?

---

2. What type of insurance does she have?

---

3. What is one of the benefits Maria has?

---

4. How does Maria feel about her benefits?

Exercise 5- Read the text below before answering the questions.

Employee Rights

Ahmed joins a union for protection. He learns about his rights at work. He can take breaks during the day. He feels safe at work.

Comprehension Questions:

1. What does Ahmed learn about?

____

2. What can he do during the day?

____

3. What does he join for protection?

____

4. How does Ahmed feel about his rights?

____

Exercise 6- Read the job ad below before answering the questions.

Job Ad

Job	Wages	Benefits	Union Fee
Warehouse Worker	$18 per hour	Health insurance, 401k	$10 per month

Comprehension Questions:

1. What is the job listed in the ad?

____

2. How much are the wages per hour?

____

3. What are two benefits mentioned?

____

4. How much is the union fee per month?

____

Employee Rights and Union Protections

Right	Explanation
Fair Wages	Workers are paid a good amount of money for the work they do.
Safe Work Environment	Workplaces must be safe and clean.
Breaks During Work	Workers can take breaks.
Join a Union	Workers can join a union for protection.

Comprehension Questions:

1. What does "fair wages" mean?

____

2. Why is a "safe work environment" important?

____

3. What can workers do during the day?

____

4. What group can workers join for protection?

____

Pay Stub

Item	Amount
Gross Salary	$3,000
Taxes	-$500
Insurance Premium	-$100
Pension	-$200
Net Pay	$2,200

Comprehension Questions:

1. What is the gross salary?

____

2. How much is taken out for taxes?

____

3. What is the final net pay?

____

4. What other deductions are listed besides taxes?

____

Letter from HR About Sick and Vacation Leave

Sunnyvale Enterprises
Human Resources Department
136 Main Street
Sunnyvale, CA 94086

October 7, 2024
Dear Employee,
We want to remind you about our sick and vacation leave policy. If you are sick, please call your supervisor. You can take up to 5 sick days a year. For vacation leave, please tell us 2 weeks before you plan to take time off. You can take 10 vacation days each year.

Thank you,
HR Department

Comprehension Questions:

1. How many sick days can an employee take?

____

2. Who should you call if you are sick?

____

3. How much notice is needed for vacation leave?

____

4. How many vacation days can an employee take each year?

____

Exercise 10- Fill in the blanks with the correct words (*rights, wages, union, pay stub, benefits*).

1. I earn my _______ every two weeks for my work.

2. My job offers health _______ for my family.

3. All workers have _______ to a safe workplace.

4. A _______ helps me understand my pay.

5. I pay a small fee to be part of the _______.

Exercise 11- Complete the sentences with words you learned in this lesson.

1. The _______ shows how much money is earned each month.

2. A good job has many _______ like vacation time.

3. The _______ helps protect my job rights.

4. Workers should always know their _______ at work.

5. My _______ is higher if I work more hours.

Exercise 12- Dictation

Your teacher will read some of the new words from Exercise 2. Write down what you hear.

____

____

ANSWER KEYS

Exercise 2- Vocabulary Matching:

1. Wages - Money earned for work
2. Deduction – Money taken out of your pay
3. Rights - Things you are allowed to do at work
4. Union - A group that helps protect workers
5. Paystub - A paper showing how much money you made

Exercise 3- Text 1:

1. Luis works at a restaurant.
2. He earns $14 per hour.
3. He feels happy.
4. He wants to save it.

Exercise 4- Text 2:

1. Maria gets benefits.
2. She has health insurance.
3. She gets vacation days.
4. She feels thankful.

Exercise 5- Text 3:

1. Ahmed learns about his rights.
2. He can take breaks.
3. He joins a union for protection.
4. He feels safe.

Exercise 6- Job Ad:

1. The job title is warehouse worker.
2. It is $18 per hour.
3. Health insurance and 401k are benefits mentioned.
4. The union fee is $10 per month.

Exercise 7- Employee Rights and Union Protections:

1. It means that workers are paid a good amount of money for the work they do.
2. It keeps workers safe.
3. Workers can take breaks.
4. Workers can join a union.

Exercise 8- Pay Stub:

1. The gross salary is $3,000.
2. $500 is taken out.
3. The final net pay is $2,200.
4. The insurance premium and pension are listed.

Exercise 9- Letter from HR:

1. An employee can take 5 sick days.
2. You should call the supervisor.
3. 2 weeks' notice is needed.
4. They can take 10 vacation days.

Exercise 10- Fill-in-the-Blanks:
1. wages
2. benefits
3. rights
4. pay stub
5. union

Exercise 11- Complete the Sentences:

1. pay stub
2. benefits
3. union
4. rights
5. salary

Lesson 3: Job performance and Training

Objectives:

- Students will read short texts and answer questions about job performance and training.
- Students will use new words to complete sentences about job skills, training sessions, and evaluations.

Exercise 1- What do you see in the pictures?

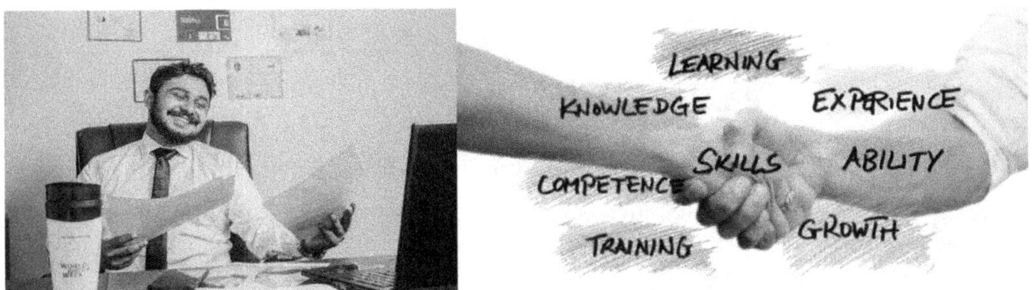

Exercise 2- Draw a line connecting each word to its meaning.

Word	Meaning
Training	How well you do your job
Performance	Things you are good at for a job
Evaluation	Comments to help you do better
Skills	A time to learn new skills
Feedback	A meeting to talk about how you work

Exercise 3- Read the text below before answering the questions.

Training Session

James goes to a training session. He learns about new safety rules. He asks questions during the class. James enjoys learning new things.

Comprehension Questions:

1. Where does James go?

____

2. What does he learn about?

____

3. What does James do during the class?

____

4. How does James feel about the training session?

____

Practicing Job Skills

Lisa practices her computer skills at work. She learns to type faster. She uses these skills to help customers. Lisa is proud of her work.

Comprehension Questions:

1. What does Lisa practice at work?

____

2. What does she learn?

____

3. How does she use these skills?

____

4. How does Lisa feel about her skills?

____

Receiving Feedback

Miguel talks to his boss. His boss gives him feedback. Miguel listens carefully to improve his work. He is happy to learn how to do better.

Comprehension Questions:

1. Who is talking with Miguel?

2. What does Miguel receive?

3. Why does Miguel listen carefully?

4. How does Miguel feel about the feedback?

Exercise 6- Read the training schedule below before answering the questions.

Monthly In-Person Training

Date	Training Topic	Time
March 15	Customer Service	10:00 AM
April 20	Safety Rules	2:00 PM
May 10	Teamwork	1:00 PM

Comprehension Questions:

1. What day is the customer service training?

2. What is the topic of the training on April 20?

3. What time is the teamwork training?

4. How many training sessions are listed?

Exercise 7- Read the training list below before answering the questions.

Mandatory Training:

Training	Description
Workplace Safety	How to stay safe at work
Computer Basics	Learn to use a computer
Customer Service	How to talk to customers

Comprehension Questions:

1. What training helps you stay safe at work?

____

2. What can you learn in Computer Basics?

____

3. What training teaches you to talk to customers?

____

4. How many mandatory training sessions are listed?

____

Exercise 8- Read the evaluation schedule below before answering the questions.

Quarterly Performance Evaluation Schedule

Quarter	Evaluation Month	Details
Q1	March	Meet with supervisor
Q2	June	Review work goals
Q3	September	Talk about skills
Q4	December	Set new goals

Comprehension Questions:

1. When is the first evaluation?

____

2. What is reviewed in the June evaluation?

____

3. Who meets with you in the March evaluation?

____

4. What is the focus of the December evaluation?

____

Blue Horizon Industries
Human Resources Department
456 Oakwood Avenue
Riverside, TX 77002

October 11, 2024
Dear Employee,
Training is very important for your job. It helps you learn new skills and improve your work. We have monthly training sessions to help you do your best. Please attend all training to become better at your job.

Thank you,
HR Department

Comprehension Questions:

1. Who wrote the letter?

____

2. Why is training important?

____

3. How often are training sessions?

____

4. What should employees do to become better?

____

1. I go to _______ to learn new skills.

2. My _______ at work is good because I practice.

3. I get an _______ to talk about my work.

4. I have computer ________ that help me do my job.

5. My boss gives me ________ to help me improve.

Exercise 11- Complete the sentences with words you learned in this lesson.

1. My job ________ is better after I practice.

2. I learn new ________ to help me in my job.

3. I attend all ________ sessions to learn more.

4. During the ________, my work is reviewed.

5. I listen to ________ from my boss to improve.

Exercise 12- Dictation

Your teacher will read some of the new words from Exercise 2. Write down what you hear.

____

____

ANSWER KEYS

Exercise 2- Vocabulary Matching:
1. Training - A time to learn new skills
2. Performance - How well you do your job
3. Evaluation - A meeting to talk about how you work
4. Skills - Things you are good at for a job
5. Feedback - Comments to help you do better

Exercise 3- Text 1:
1. James goes to a training session.
2. He learns about new safety rules.
3. He asks questions.
4. He enjoys learning.

Exercise 4- Text 2:
1. Lisa practices her computer skills.
2. She learns to type faster.
3. She uses them to help customers.
4. She is proud.

Exercise 5- Text 3:
1. Miguel's boss is talking with him.
2. He receives feedback.
3. He listens to improve his work.
4. He feels happy.

Exercise 6- Training Schedule:
1. It is on March 15.
2. The topic is "Safety Rules."
3. The teamwork training is at 1:00 PM.
4. Three sessions are listed.

Exercise 7- Mandatory Training List:
1. Workplace safety helps you stay safe.
2. You can learn to use a computer.
3. Customer service trains you with this.
4. Three sessions are listed.

Exercise 8- Evaluation Schedule:
1. The first one is in March.
2. Work goals are reviewed.
3. The supervisor meets with you.
4. Setting new goals is the focus.

Exercise 9- Letter from HR:
1. The HR department wrote the letter.
2. It helps you learn new skills and improve.
3. They are monthly.
4. They should attend all sessions.

Exercise 10- Fill-in-the-Blanks:
1. training
2. performance
3. evaluation
4. skills
5. feedback

Exercise 11- Complete the Sentences:
1. performance
2. skills
3. training
4. evaluation
5. feedback

Lesson 4: Communicating at the Workplace

Objectives:

1. Students will read short texts and answer questions about effective communication in the workplace.
2. Students will use new words to complete sentences about how to communicate well with coworkers and managers.

Exercise 1- What do you see in the pictures?

Exercise 2- Draw a line connecting each word to its meaning.

Word	Meaning
Listen	A message sent on a computer
Speak	A device used to talk to others
Email	To hear and understand someone
Message	To say words out loud
Phone	Information shared with someone

Exercise 3- Read the text below before answering the questions.

Talking to Coworkers

Ben talks to his coworkers. They share ideas for a project. Ben listens carefully. He likes working with his team.

Comprehension Questions:

1. Who does Ben talk to?

2. What do they share?

____

3. How does Ben listen?

____

4. How does Ben feel about working with his team?

____

Sending an Email

Sara sends an email to her boss. She writes clearly. She asks questions about her work. Sara checks her email every day.

Comprehension Questions:

1. Who does Sara send an email to?

____

2. What does she ask in the email?

____

3. How does she write her email?

____

4. How often does Sara check her email?

____

Talking on the Phone

David talks on the phone at work. He calls a customer. He speaks slowly and clearly. The customer thanks him for his help.

Comprehension Questions:

1. Who does David talk to on the phone?

____

2. How does David speak?

____

3. Why does David call the customer?

____

4. What does the customer say to David?

____

Exercise 6- Read the communication tips below before answering the questions.

Email Communication Tips

Tip	Advice
Be clear.	Use short sentences.
Be polite.	Use "please" and "thank you."
Check spelling.	Look for mistakes before sending messages.

Comprehension Questions:

1. What kind of sentences should you write?

____

2. What words should you use to be polite?

____

3. What should you check before sending an email?

____

4. How many tips are listed?

____

Communication Training

Training	Purpose
Email Skills	Learn to write professional emails.
Phone Etiquette	Learn to speak politely on the phone.
Team Communication	Practice talking in a team.

Comprehension Questions:

1. What training helps with writing emails?

____

2. What can you learn in phone etiquette training?

____

3. Which training focuses on talking with a team?

____

4. How many communication trainings are listed?

____

Phone Communication Practices

Practice	How to Do It
Speak clearly.	Talk slowly and use simple words.
Listen carefully.	Pay attention to the other person.
Use good manners.	Say "please" and "thank you."

Comprehension Questions:

1. How should you speak on the phone?

____

2. What should you do when listening?

____

3. What words show good manners?

____

4. What should you pay attention to when listening?

____

Maplewood Solutions
Human Resources Department
789 Pinecrest Boulevard
Maplewood, FL 32801

September 27, 2024
Dear Employee,
Communication is very important at work. Good communication helps you work well with others. Please remember to speak clearly, listen carefully, and be polite. This will help you be a better team member.

Thank you,
HR Department

Comprehension Questions:

1. Which company sent this letter?

____

2. Why is communication important?

____

3. What should you do when you speak?

____

4. What will good communication help you be?

____

1. I need to _______ carefully to my boss.

2. I use the _______ to talk to customers.

3. I _______ to my coworker about the project.

4. I write an _______ to my supervisor.

5. I leave a _______ for my friend about the meeting

Exercise 11- Complete the sentences with words you learned in this lesson.

1. I check my _______ every morning for new messages.

2. I _______ when my boss talks to me.

3. I _______ on the phone with customers.

4. My friend left me a _______ about the team meeting.

5. I write an _______ to ask a question.

ANSWER KEYS

Exercise 2- Vocabulary Matching:

1. Listen - To hear and understand someone
2. Speak - To say words out loud
3. Email - A message sent on a computer
4. Message - Information shared with someone
5. Phone - A device used to talk to others

Exercise 3- Text 1:

1. He talks to his coworkers.
2. They share ideas for a project.
3. He listens carefully.
4. Ben likes working with the team.

Exercise 4- Text 2:

1. She sends an email to her boss.
2. She asks questions about work.
3. She writes clearly.
4. She checks it every day.

Exercise 5- Text 3:

1. He talks to a customer.
2. He speaks slowly and clearly.
3. He calls to help the customer.
4. The customer thanks him for his help.

Exercise 6- Communication Tips:

1. You should write short sentences.
2. You should use "please" and "thank you".
3. You should check your spelling.
4. Three tips are listed.

Exercise 7- Communication Training List:

1. "Email Skills" helps with this.
2. You can learn to speak politely on the phone.
3. "Team Communication" focuses on talking with a team.
4. Three types of training are listed.

Exercise 8- Phone Communication Practices:

1. You should speak clearly and use simple words.
2. You should pay attention.
3. "Please" and "thank you" show good manners.
4. You should pay attention to the other person.

Exercise 9- Letter from HR:

1. The letter is from Maplewood Solutions.
2. It helps you work well with others.
3. You should speak clearly.
4. It will help you be a better team member.

Exercise 10- Fill-in-the-Blanks:

1. listen
2. phone
3. speak
4. email
5. message

Exercise 11- Complete the Sentences:

1. email
2. listen
3. speak
4. message
5. email

REFLECTION ON LEARNING

Answer the following questions and discuss your responses with your teacher or classmates.

1. What reading strategies did you learn or practice in this unit?

2. What new words did you learn?

3. What reading challenges did you face?

4. What reading strategies do you need to improve?

5. What do you want your teacher to know?

UNIT 6: GOVERNMENT AND LAW

Objectives:

1. Students will read short texts and answer questions about government and law.
2. Students will use new words to complete sentences about different levels of government and law enforcement.

Exercise 1- What do you see in the pictures?

Exercise 2- Draw a line connecting each word to its meaning.

Word	Meaning
Law	A person who leads a city or town
Government	To choose a leader or make a decision
Vote	People who keep the community safe
Police	A rule that people must follow
Mayor	A group that makes laws and helps the country

Exercise 3- Read the text below before answering the questions.

Police in the Community

Officer Kim helps in the community. She talks to people about safety. She drives around the neighborhood. People feel safe when they see Officer Kim.

Comprehension Questions:

1. Who helps in the community?

2. What does Officer Kim talk about?

3. What does she do around the neighborhood?

4. How do people feel when they see Officer Kim?

Voting in an Election

Maria votes in an election. She goes to the voting place with her friend. Maria chooses a leader for her city. She is thankful to vote.

Comprehension Questions:

1. What does Maria do in the election?

2. Where does she go to vote?

3. What does Maria choose?

4. How does Maria feel about voting?

A Mayor Working for the City

Mayor John works for the city. He makes plans for parks and schools. He talks to the people in the city. He wants to make the city a better place.

Comprehension Questions:

1. What is Mayor John's job?

____

2. What plans does he make?

____

3. Who does the mayor talk to?

____

4. What does the mayor want to do for the city?

____

Federal, State, and Local Government

Government Level	What They Do
Federal	Makes laws for the whole country
State	Makes laws for the state and schools
Local	Helps with city things like parks and roads

Comprehension Questions:

1. What does the federal government do?

____

2. Which level makes laws for the state?

____

3. What does the local government help with?

____

4. How many government levels are listed?

____

Law Enforcement

Role	What They Do
Police	Keep people safe, make sure people follow the law, and help in emergencies
Sheriff	Protects the county and makes sure people follow the law
FBI Agent	Works to protect the country from big crimes

Comprehension Questions:

1. What is the main job of the police?

____

2. Who protects the county?

____

3. Who works on big crimes in the country?

____

4. Which groups make sure people follow the law?

____

Elected Officials and Their Roles

Official	What They Do
Mayor	Leads the city and makes plans
Governor	Leads the state and makes laws
President	Leads the country and signs laws

Comprehension Questions:

1. Who leads the city?

____

2. Who makes laws for the state?

____

3. Who signs laws for the country?

____

4. Which official leads the country?

____

Exercise 9- Fill in the blanks with the correct words (*vote, police, law, government, mayor*).

1. The _______ helps make laws for the country.

2. I _______ for my favorite leader in the election.

3. The _______ makes sure everyone follows the law.

4. The _______ is the leader of the city.

5. A _______ is a rule that we must all follow.

Exercise 10- Complete the sentences with words you learned in this lesson.

1. It is important to follow the _______.

2. The _______ signs laws for the country.

3. I want to _______ in the next election.

4. The _______ protects the citizens from big crimes.

5. Our _______ is working to improve city parks.

Exercise 11- Dictation

Your teacher will read some of the new words from Exercise 2. Write down what you hear.

____

____

ANSWER KEYS

Exercise 2- Vocabulary Matching:

1. Law - A rule that people must follow
2. Government - A group that makes laws and helps the country
3. Vote - To choose a leader or make a decision
4. Police - People who keep the community safe
5. Mayor - A person who leads a city or town

Exercise 3- Text 1:

1. Officer Kim helps in the community.
2. She talks about safety.
3. She drives around.
4. They feel safe.

Exercise 4- Text 2:

1. She votes.
2. She goes to the voting place.
3. She chooses the leader of the city.
4. She is thankful to vote.

Exercise 5- Text 3:

1. He works for the city.
2. He makes plans for parks and schools.
3. He talks to the people in the city.
4. He wants to make the city better.

Exercise 6- Federal, State, and Local Government:

1. The federal government makes laws for the country.
2. State government makes laws for the state.
3. Local government helps with parks and roads.
4. Three levels are listed.

Exercise 7- Law Enforcement:

1. The police keep people safe.
2. The sheriff protects the county.
3. The FBI agent works on big crimes.
4. The police and sheriff make sure people follow the law.

Exercise 8- Elected Officials:

1. The mayor leads the city.
2. The governor makes laws for the state.
3. The President signs laws for the country.
4. The President leads the country.

Exercise 9- Fill-in-the-Blanks:

1. government
2. vote
3. police
4. mayor
5. law

Exercise 10- Complete the Sentences:

1. law
2. President
3. vote
4. FBI
5. mayor

REFLECTION ON LEARNING

Answer the following questions and discuss your responses with your teacher or classmates.

1. What reading strategies did you learn or practice in this unit?

2. What new words did you learn?

3. What reading challenges did you face?

4. What reading strategies do you need to improve?

5. What do you want your teacher to know?

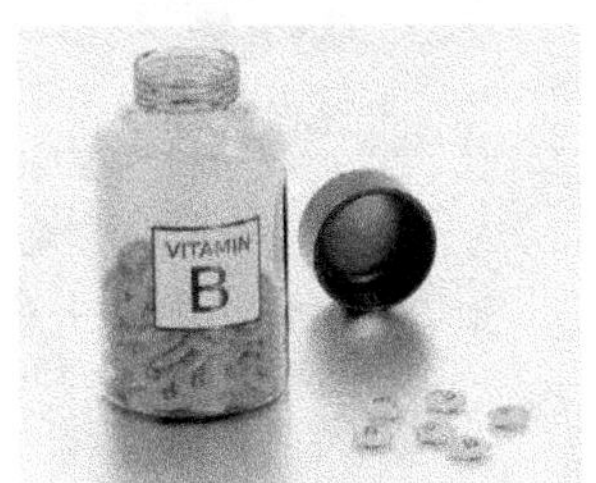

1. What is in the bottle?

    A) Medicine

    B) Water

    C) Vitamins

    D) Juice

2. The label on the bottle says:

    A) Vitamin B

    B) Vitamin D and B

    C) Orange juice

    D) Milk

Day	Temperature	Feels Like	Humidity
Sunday	25°	27°	62%
Monday	17°	15°	25%
Tuesday	33°	36°	75%
Wednesday	5°	3°	12%
Thursday	13°	14°	33%
Friday	-7°	-10°	80%
Saturday	0°	-2°	91%

3. What is the weather like on Tuesday?

    A) Rainy

    B) Sunny

    C) Cloudy

    D) Snowy

4. What is the lowest temperature shown in the forecast?

    A) 0°C

    B) 5°C

    C) -7°C

    D) 25°C

5. What day is written on the ticket?

A) Monday

C) Friday

B) Thursday

D) Sunday

6. What is the time written on the ticket?

A) 12:00

C) 14:00

B) 10:00

D) 16:00

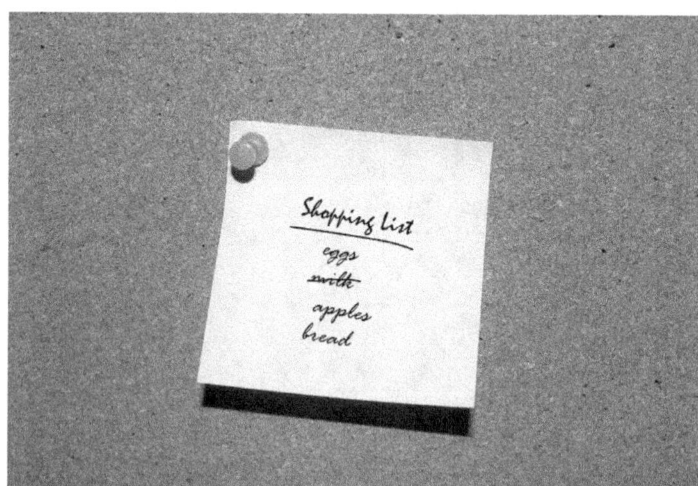

7. Which item is not on the shopping list?

A) Bread

C) Water

B) Eggs

D) Apples

8. What item is crossed off the list?

A) Apples

C) Bread

B) Milk

D) Eggs

9. What is the image advertising?

A) Summer sale

B) Winter sale

C) Halloween sale

D) Birthday sale

10. How much discount is offered?

A) Up to 20%

B) Up to 30%

C) Up to 50%

D) No discount

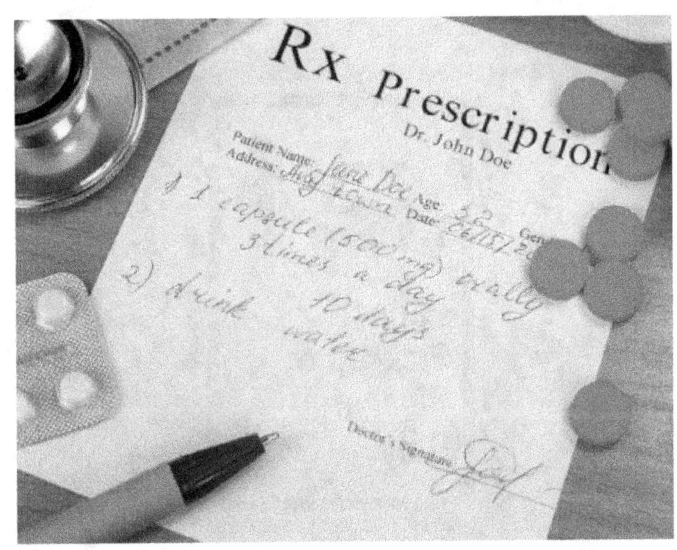

11. What does the prescription say to take?

A) 1 capsule

B) 2 capsules

C) 3 capsules

D) No medicine

12. How long should the person take the medicine?

A) 5 days

B) 7 days

C) 10 days

D) 15 days

13. What is one thing you can find at Exit 13?

A) Zoo

B) Library

C) Food

D) School

14. What service is not listed on the sign?

A) Gas

B) Phone

C) Lodging

D) Internet

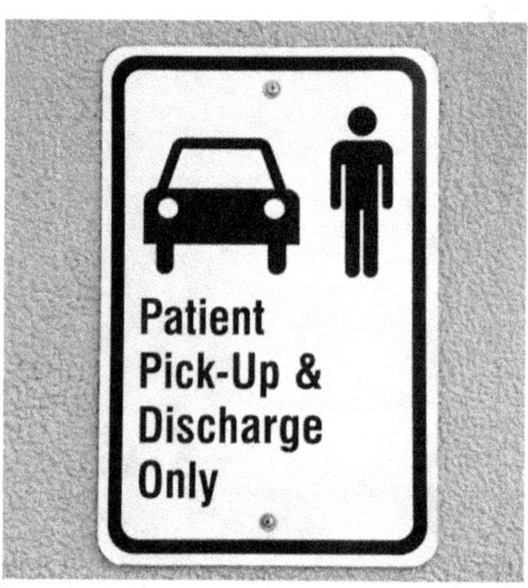

15. What is the purpose of the sign?

A) To park cars

B) To play sports

C) For patient pick-up and discharge

D) For bike parking

16. Where would you see this sign?

A) At a park

B) At a hospital

C) At a zoo

D) At a school

17. What is one employee benefit?

A) Free food

C) Free car

B) Employee discount

D) Paid vacation days

18. Which of these is an employee right?

A) Paid vacation

C) Free house

B) Birthday gift

D) Breaks during shift

19. What type of restaurant is in the image?

A) Italian

C) Sushi

B) Barbecue

D) Fast Food

20. What is written at the top of the logo?

A) Fresh & Healthy

C) Fresh & Tasty

B) Open 24/7

D) New Restaurant

21. Where is the person traveling to?

    A) Los Angeles   C) London

    B) New York   D) Paris

22. What is the date of the flight?

    A) June 15, 2021   C) April 10, 2021

    B) May 12, 2021   D) July 20, 2021

COMPUTER TRAINING CLASS

Learn essential computer skills to improve your job performance! Gain confidence using email, spreadsheets, and presentations. Affordable classes, starting next week!

23. What skills will the class teach?

    A) Cooking   C) Driving

    B) Computer skills   D) Gardening

24. When will the classes start?

    A) Next month   C) Next week

    B) Tomorrow   D) Today

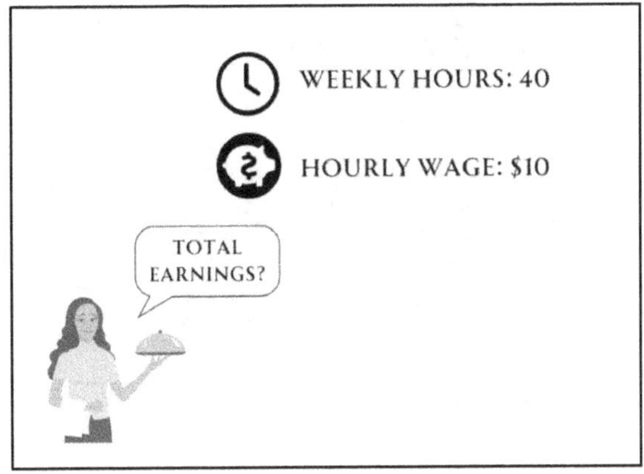

25. How many hours does the person work weekly?

A) 10 hours

B) 20 hours

C) 30 hours

D) 40 hours

26. What is the hourly wage?

A) $5

B) $15

C) $10

D) $20

27. Who is welcome to rent the rooms?

A) Tourists

B) Students

C) Immigrants

D) Business travelers

28. What is the main purpose of the sign?

A) To sell houses

B) To find roommates

C) To rent rooms

D) To give directions

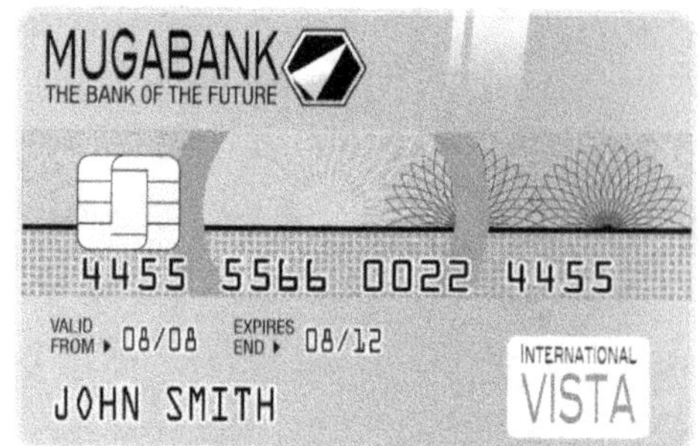

29. What is the name of the bank on the card?

A) WorldBank

C) MugaBank

B) Bank of America

D) Global Bank

30. Whose name is on the credit card?

A) Jane Doe

C) Robert Brown

B) John Smith

D) Lisa White

31. What kind of program is on the poster?

A) Housing assistance

C) Medical aid

B) Unemployment benefits

D) Food assistance

32. What is the purpose of the program?

A) To help families get healthy foods

B) To help families with housing

C) To help people who have lost their jobs

D) To help people pay for their health care

CARLOS RAMIREZ
MONTHLY BUDGET

MONTH: AUGUST   **YEAR: 2024**

MONTHLY EXPENSES

Rent	$800
Groceries	$400
Transportation	$150
Utilities	$200
Total	**$1550**

SALARY

$2000

SAVINGS

$450

33. How much does Carlos earn every month??

A) $2100

B) $2200

C) $2000

D) $2300

34. What is Carlos' total monthly expenses?

A) $1500

B) $1550

C) $1600

D) $1650

ANSWER KEYS

1. C	10. C	18. D	27. C
2. A	11. A	19. B	28. C
3. B	12. C	20. C	29. C
4. C	13. C	21. C	30. B
5. B	14. D	22. B	31. D
6. C	15. C	23. B	32. A
7. C	16. B	24. C	33. C
8. B	17. D	25. D	34. B
9. B		26. C	

REFLECTION ON LEARNING

Answer the following questions and discuss your responses with your teacher or classmates.

1. How do you feel about your performance on the practice test?

2. Was anything too hard for you? What was it?

3. Was anything too easy for you? What was it?

4. What reading strategies do you still need to review?

5. What else do you want your teacher to know?

ADULT ED
MATH
NUMBER SYSTEM, NUMBER SENSE, AND OPERATIONS PREPARING
FOR
CASAS, TABE 11 & 12, HISET, AND GED TESTING
BY COACHING FOR BETTER LEARNING

ADULT ED
MATH
GEOMETRY PREPARING
FOR
CASAS, TABE 11 & 12, HISET, AND GED TESTING
BY COACHING FOR BETTER LEARNING

CBL COACHING
Math
Practice Worksheets and Workbook for Adult Students

SKILLS FOR SUCCESS IN CAREER AND TECHNICAL EDUCATION (CTE)
STUDENT GUIDE
A SYSTEMATIC WAY TO MASTER ORGANIZATIONAL AND SOFT SKILLS
CBL COACHING

HOW TO ACHIEVE BETTER STUDENT RETENTION IN ADULT EDUCATION
TEDDY EDOUARD

TABE 11 & 12
CONSUMABLE STUDENT READING MANUAL
FOR LEVEL E
By Coaching for Better Learning, LLC

TABE 11 & 12
CONSUMABLE STUDENT READING MANUAL
FOR LEVEL M
By Coaching for Better Learning, LLC

TABE 11 & 12
CONSUMABLE STUDENT READING MANUAL
FOR LEVEL D
By Coaching for Better Learning, LLC

TABE 11 & 12
STUDENT LANGUAGE MANUAL
FOR LEVEL E
By Coaching for Better Learning, LLC

TABE 11 & 12
STUDENT LANGUAGE MANUAL
FOR LEVEL M
By Coaching for Better Learning, LLC

Preparing Adult Learners for TABE 11 & 12 Math Tests and for Vocational Training Entrance Math Exams
TABE 11 & 12
Consumable Student Math Workbook
FOR LEVEL E
By Coaching for Better Learning, LLC

Preparing Adult Learners for TABE 11 & 12 Math Tests and for Vocational Training Entrance Math Exams
TABE 11 & 12
Consumable Student Math Workbook
FOR LEVEL M
By Coaching for Better Learning, LLC

Preparing Adult Learners for TABE 11 & 12 Math Tests and for Vocational Training Entrance Math Exams
TABE 11 & 12
Consumable Student Math Workbook
FOR LEVEL D
By Coaching for Better Learning, LLC

Preparing Adult Learners for TABE 11 & 12 Math Tests and for Vocational Training Entrance Math Exams
TABE 11 & 12
Consumable Student Math Workbook
FOR LEVEL A
By Coaching for Better Learning, LLC

CBL COACHING
Workbook
Number and Letter Tracing for Adult Students
This tool is designed to help adult students practice and master handwriting. It is appropriate for Literacy, ESL, and ABE classes.

READING NOTEBOOK & JOURNAL
For Adult Students
By Coaching For Better Learning   CBL COACHING

MATH NOTEBOOK & JOURNAL
For Adult Students
By Coaching For Better Learning   CBL COACHING

BOOK 1
PHONICS AND LIFE SKILLS READING
FOR
Adult Literacy, ABE, and ESL Students
Turning Learners into Proficient Readers
CBL COACHING FOR BETTER LEARNING

BOOK 2
PHONICS AND LIFE SKILLS READING
FOR
Adult Literacy, ABE, and ESL Students
Turning Learners into Proficient Readers
CBL COACHING FOR BETTER LEARNING

BOOK 3
PHONICS AND LIFE SKILLS READING
FOR
Adult Literacy, ABE, and ESL Students
Turning Learners into Proficient Readers
CBL COACHING FOR BETTER LEARNING

ABOUT CBL

At CBL, we promote systematic solutions, learner-centered textbooks, and forward-thinking strategies in adult education, workforce development, and vocational training. Our diverse solutions and products are intricately designed to enrich students' learning experiences while making the job of busy, hard-working adult instructors easier.

CBL takes pride in publishing student-centered textbooks designed to prepare learners for CASAS, TABE 11&12, HiSET, and GED assessments and to assist instructors in covering course curricula and standards with confidence.

Our publications also include teaching guides, test prep tools, and study guides that foster reflective learning, ensuring sustained engagement in active learning. Find our meticulously crafted textbooks on our book page (cbledu.com) or major platforms like Amazon, Barnes & Noble, and Ingram Spark.

CBL also guides adult education and workforce programs in establishing robust professional development programs—training, peer-mentoring, coaching, community of practices (CoPs), and instructional systems— fostering a culture of continuous improvement and contributing to higher learner retention and success rates. We also offer workshops and PD sessions for adult educators and classroom instructors.

If you have questions about instructional systems, textbooks, or student learning and retention, contact us today at teamcbl@cbledu.com or 410-960-4082.

www.ingramcontent.com/pod-product-compliance
Lightning Source LLC
Chambersburg PA
CBHW080743120726
48001CB00009B/2669